Helping Children Learn: Contributions to a Cognitive Curriculum

Sara Meadows and Asher Cashdan

David Fulton Publishers
London

David Fulton Publishers Ltd
14 Chalton Drive London N2 0QW

First published in Great Britain by
David Fulton Publishers 1988

British Library Cataloguing in Publication Data

Meadows, Sara
  Helping children learn.
  1. Learning by children
  I. Title   II. Cashdan, Asher
  155.4′13

  ISBN 1-85346-060-5

Typeset by Chapterhouse, Formby
Printed in Great Britain by
St Edmundsbury Press Ltd, Bury St Edmunds, Suffolk

Contents

Acknowledgements

The contents of this book are based on more than ten years of work in nursery schools and discussion with teachers. We are glad to acknowledge the financial support of the Social Science Research Council, grant no. HR 3456 'Teaching Styles in Nursery Education', project directors Asher Cashdan and Janet Philps. The work of Janet Philps, Ronny Flynn, Jenny Weaver and the teachers involved in this study has contributed a great deal to our understanding of teaching young children, as has that of Christianne Hayward. We are also grateful for illuminating discussions with Kathy Sylva, Philip Gammage, Stephen Tyler, Barbara Tizard, Gordon Wells, Peter Robinson, Belle Tutaev, Martin Hughes, Peter Smith, Lynn Michell, Ruth Burberry, Marion Wilson, Christine Rudge, Joy Donovan, Julia Cloke, Martin Woodhead, Mary Fawcett, and others. Our thanks to Valerie Mitchell, Fiona Harrison and Maureen Harvey for secretarial work.

Foreword

Twenty years after the publication of the Plowden Report seemed to be a proper period for some assessment of the state of affairs in Primary Schooling, and the series of which this volume is a member arose from consideration of progress since that report. Powerful in its presentation and comprehensive in its coverage, the Plowden Report was also distinctive. Its predecessors appeared to rely mainly upon their Committee's sampling of presumed informed opinion for their recommendations. In contrast, the Plowden Committee conducted national surveys to obtain answers to some empirical questions and took this kind of evidence into account in formulating recommendations about policy. Further, the authors of the report attempted to portray the psychological development of the child as a coherent frame of reference to which to relate the curriculum.

Alas, this precedent of attempting to establish a sound conceptual framework and an appropriate research base on which to found educational decisions has not been the hallmark of subsequent government reports or policies. Neither has there been a subsequent review of Plowden's proposals and assumptions.

Which psychological principles of Plowden have been applied and found to be efficient and desirable? Which psychological principles of Plowden have not been applied or have been misapplied and with what consequences? Which principles have been tried and found to be wrong, perhaps making assumptions about children which are just not true? A variety of questions of this kind can be asked, and if we are to follow Plowden's prescriptions we have to 'find out' for ourselves what the most likely answers are. Research in the social sciences is relevant, and a main function of this series is to review the state of evidence about some of the Plowden statements, twenty years on.

Sara Meadows and Asher Cashdan do this in respect of some major assumptions about the role of play and talk in the development of young children. The analysis of her own research and that of others shows under what conditions what kinds of play and talk are likely to be associated with development as well as pleasure. Plowden's own notions about these activities were perhaps optimistically simple and when put into practice became simplified further and to a degree that did little to promote development.

Perhaps 'play is the principal means of learning in early childhood', but some kinds of play are more efficacious than others. Likewise, although it may now be a firm conviction that 'spoken language plays a central role in learning' (some learning at least), and that 'the development of language is central to the educational process', we have to ask how much of what kinds of language experience in what contexts does promote development? The authors demonstrate that we have made relevant progress in our knowledge and understanding about these matters since 1967. Finally, with their third theme of books and their possibilities, they develop some of the ideas of Plowden about reading which became over-simplified in too many of the country's classrooms.

The volume shows that psychologists in collaboration with teachers have generated research which can be exploited for progress rather than change, adding to and supplanting some of the assumptions and beliefs of not very long ago. We are pleased to make these advances available both to teachers in training and to those serving teachers who wish to know what progress has been made that might now inform their practice.

Peter Robinson
September 1988

CHAPTER 1

Introduction

The concern of this book is how we may help young children learn in nursery schools and similar settings. We do not present an entirely new curriculum for early childhood education, for the good reason that there is much that is excellent in the existing curriculum. Nor do we offer a theory of how young children learn that is radically different from earlier theories, for similar reasons. What we are proposing is a shift in emphasis in both curriculum and the theory that justifies it. We are doing so because we believe that what is normally done in nursery schools and classes (and in playgroups and in infant school reception classes) is enjoyable and useful but not, perhaps, quite fulfilling our high hopes for its educational potential.

We are in full sympathy with the long-standing and important aims of early childhood education: to facilitate the social, physical, intellectual, cultural and emotional development of children; to enhance and complement the contributions of their homes; to ready them for the years of compulsory schooling; to begin to ameliorate the effects of disadvantage. We regard these as part of what should be one of society's highest priorities – the care and education of its youngest members. Undoubtedly nursery teachers are making an important contribution to these goals. They are doing so in a spirit of warm commitment, busily doing marvels of creativity with limited resources, lovingly supporting children and families under stress despite the considerable strain of their responsibility for twenty or thirty active small children. Their job would certainly be made easier if there were, simply, more staff and less need to 'make do and mend', though staff management takes up time and teachers rightly take pride in their creative improvisations – the '1001 things to do with an eggbox' game! However, even without the improvements in resources and prestige which we would like to see, we think there are things not at present often done which, used more widely, could enhance children's experience in the nursery classroom. The aim of this book is to present two possible extensions of the traditional early childhood curriculum, justifying their usefulness by looking at what goes on in the ordinary nursery regime and what effects can be seen, and at ideas about young children and their learning.

Both our proposed innovations have long pedigrees, and bear some resemblance to elements of 'normal good practice'. This is as it should be. Apart from innovations dependent on new technology and science, most creativity in education (and elsewhere) involves a more harmonious rearrangement of things that were already known about. It is the reader's job to consider our suggestions rather than to say 'we already do that'. It may be useful to compare what 'we already do' with what has worked well elsewhere, and, in the case of our two curriculum innovations, has been evaluated rather more systematically than practitioners can easily do in day-to-day practice.

Both our innovations involve language, but not with the development of language skills as a main or only goal. We are firmly committed to the view that language is a crucial tool for learning for 3–5 year olds, as it is for older children and adults, but that does not mean we ought to be concentrating solely on teaching children about language or even how to use it. We want to see not children acquiring more and better language for its own sake but children using language for important purposes and, in so doing, improving their language skills. Sometimes, certainly, there is need to stop the use and look at the tools and how they are being used, but then this should be done explicitly. Objectives for the teacher should be offered as objectives for the child. Too many covert intentions, too much 'hidden curriculum', will be demoralising for all concerned and may make the intended learning less likely.

We are recommending curriculum innovations that have at their core two specialised uses of language – the tutorial dialogue and the enjoyment of literature. These may be unfamiliar ways of using language for some children. We do not associate ourselves with those who regard 'unfamiliar' as meaning 'deficit'. Very few children have defective language development, as we discuss later. Some are well-practised in answering display questions; others may be more familiar with using language to tease and tell jokes. Some may never have lacked a book to look at and an adult to read it to them; others may not have been read to or told stories. Almost all can, nevertheless, use language in much the same range of different ways. If they do not show their competence in school, this does not necessarily mean that it is altogether lacking. The differences in their earlier experience lead to differences in what use they can at first make of school's facilities, not to broad linguistic or cognitive deficits in and beyond education. The task of the teacher is to make sure that children's experience of the classroom does not deter them from using language at least as competently as they do elsewhere. We will see later that there is evidence that it is difficult for teachers to do this, that many teacher–child conversations are artificial, mundane or fragmentary. Our curriculum innovations help get round this problem and do facilitate better language use. As we said earlier, however, their main focus is not teaching language. Tutorial dialogue and literacy are crucial components of later education, and some early familiarisation may perhaps be helpful, particularly for children nearing their entry into compulsory schooling. However, we see the main value of our innovations as being in their allowing a more fruitful interchange between teaching and learning, two activities whose relatedness has recently come to be seen in a new way.

The 'transmission' model of teaching and learning dominated much of formal education, even the education of young children, until relatively recently. Children were there to be told: if they were told, they should then know. Failure to learn could then be attributed to the child's laziness or inattention or poor ability, or to poor transmission on the part of the teacher. Such a model was realised physically in the arrangement of the classroom - quiet children sitting in neat rows, all facing the one, talking, teacher. The larger their ears and the better they were pointed in the right direction, the more successfully they would learn what the teacher was teaching, or so the model said. In the latter part of the nineteenth century, 3–5 year olds were taught like this, and of course some education is provided like this still. In early childhood education, however, the transmission model gave way to a much more child-centred view of the learning process, dominant now for the last forty or fifty years. Here the responsibility for actions leading to learning is transferred very largely to the children themselves. The teacher's role is seen to be that of guide, friend, counsellor, facilitator. Teacher intervention should be of the gentlest kind, the teacher's main skill lying in the provision of appropriate materials for learning, and the structuring of the classroom context, both social and intellectual, so as to make learning more likely and attractive. Any intervention should follow careful observation of the child's spontaneous activities and should typically involve suggestions for the use of particular material, such as a new way of playing with water which will help the child leave an unproductive or repetitive routine or take up a new opportunity.

While this is a more appealing model than the transmission one, so far as early childhood education is concerned, both models deny the teacher a full role in the most demanding aspect of assisting in a child's education, that of operating at a high level of skill as a teacher. This is because both models are one sided, the two separate aspects of what is really a twin process (as English terminology obscures by contrasting 'teaching' and 'learning', but Russian underlines by using the word *'obuchenie'* for both). Both are essentially soft options. It is extremely easy to stand in front of people and tell them things if you assume that their failure to remember or act on what you have transmitted is their fault not yours. It is also comparatively easy to provide a fertile environment and make it the responsibility of the learner to grow in it. To take on a fair share of the whole teaching–learning process, to teach somebody something that they do not already know, is really rather difficult. Close observation of what happens in classrooms has suggested that it doesn't happen all that often. Either the task proves so easy that the pupil can successfully perform it already, and it may be the teacher who has learned (about the pupil's skills) rather than the pupil; or the task proves so difficult that only an enormous amount of teacher skill and time will help the pupil to succeed at it. In the first situation the teacher's professional skills are irrelevant; in the second they are certainly necessary but the pressures of classroom life all too often mean they cannot be deployed successfully.

We are concerned to make events in the middle band more frequent and more successful. We see the best teaching and learning occurring when there are tasks correctly tailored to the child's level and need, which, with the help of an intelligent and experienced expert (that is, a trained teacher), the child can handle successfully. Teachers have the theoretical and practical knowledge of learning, of how it occurs and where it goes wrong, that enables them both to have a good sense of what the learner is doing and to adjust the learning task and its context to maximise success. Doing this is the essential core of teaching – to do less is an abdication, to do more is to risk forcing events. While we all are used to making adjustments of this sort in everyday conversation, where we automatically monitor the success of our communications, the professional skills of teachers give them an advantage over non-professionals such as parents, important though the latter are in the education of children. Parents have, ideally, the advantage of a natural context for learning, shared interests and purposes, detailed knowledge of their children, time to spend with them as individuals and an interest (sometimes too pushy an interest) in the children's achieving the goals they have set themselves. If teachers can gain some of these advantages, they can bring their professional skills to bear more fruitfully. One of the strengths of our curriculum innovations is that they provide shared context and interests, and so facilitate the 'matching' of teaching and learning.

They do so across the subject curriculum. The literary-centred curriculum is obviously an important component in learning about language, literacy and the arts, but its story centre can also serve as a motivator for scientific, mathematical and practical work. Similarly the dialogue approach has been allied to 'scientific' problem solving, offering strengths in careful observation and experimentation, but it can pervade the whole curriculum. We believe that what is needed for the best curriculum for early learning is a core of techniques and practices that allow the teacher to develop a fine-grained analysis of the strengths and needs of the children, and to train the children to satisfy these needs themselves. This means a structuring of the whole classroom environment so that it is conducive to intellectual development, a fit place for the self-running problem solvers we want the children to be; a structuring that will also enable the teacher to spend much more time facilitating the children's learning rather than managing the environment. Our approaches should be not separable parts of the curriculum but part of the whole texture of the activities and relationships shared by teacher and children.

CHAPTER 2

'Mainstream Good Practice': Is There a Discrepancy between Hope and Achievement?

The mainstay of early childhood education has been the provision of opportunities for supervised, but freely chosen, play for children. The adults concerned – teachers, nursery nurses, playgroup personnel and so forth – decide on materials and activities. They set them out and let the children choose what to play with, sometimes suggesting an activity to an underoccupied child, sometimes telling children that they must wait to take their turn with a popular activity. Adult supervision ranges from tight control over activities that children cannot manage alone, via intervention as needed to support or extend what a child is doing, to 'just keeping an eye on' activities that don't seem to need much adult attention. Most commonly it is a discreet supervision making sure that no one comes to grief. Children choose their own activities and develop them, by and large, as they themselves elect. Adults do not often direct play, though they may suggest new possibilities or keep the child's developments within the bounds set by considerations like not inconveniencing other people; they rarely play themselves, beyond a brief response to a child's invitation to join in pretend play or a little modelling of art activities such as making plasticine models. The adults have thought about what materials and activities are desirable and what their educational potential is, and try to provide both activities at the level particular children 'need' and a 'balanced menu' for the whole group. This menu is likely to include opportunities to paint and draw, to play with bricks and construction toys, to role play in a Wendy house or other setting, to do puzzles and investigative or thinking games, to play with sand, clay or water, to look at books and to play with model toys and dolls. There may also be school-like activities such as tracing or reading flashcards and craft activities such as assembling Easter Bunnies, which have more direction from adults, and opportunities for gross motor play on swings, bicycles and so forth, which are less supervised. Each day some activity is offered which could contribute to the social, physical, intellectual or emotional development of the child: children are mostly left with considerable freedom to make what they wish of these activities.

The degree of child-centredness and learner-choice that this involves is probably greater than at any other point in the education system. It may seem paradoxical that it is the least experienced learners who are left most free to choose their own learning; and the reasons for this practice are indeed complex. Historically, it has not always been so. In the late nineteenth century, many 3 and 4 year olds were taught in 'baby classes' where they sat throughout the school day in rows doing rote exercises on the '3 Rs' – if they were able to stay awake. Some early enthusiasm for free play was a reaction to this not very satisfactory curriculum. Theoretical rationales were derived from Froebel and from Susan Isaacs, and later from Piaget: we examine these models of how children learn in Chapter 4. Briefly, the idea is that young children need to have rich experience and learn from it at their own pace. Teachers are to act as sympathetic and imaginative observers, to provide advice and guidance when it is asked for, to trust the child's own sense of timing and not try to accelerate development.

This sort of approach requires the teacher to know a great deal about child development in general and each child's individual development in particular. If she is to be able to provide *appropriate* facilities, advice and guidance, she must be able to diagnose what the child can do at present and what the next thing to be learned might be, as these facts about present state and immediate potential will determine what the child should be offered next. She should also know, incidentally, quite a lot about the child's past history of learning and about what other adults may be providing, if her help is to be really on the spot. It is remarkable how good teachers can be at making these diagnoses, at making subtle choices about what to offer children or how to direct their activity. Their understanding of 'the whole child' and how to adjust the curriculum moment by moment for optimum learning can be immensely fruitful, but the demands it makes should not be underestimated. In its respect for children's creativity and autonomy, and in its denial of the competitiveness and pass/fail attitudes that increase in their effects later in the schooling of children, this is an attractive model. However, we do need to justify it in educational terms if it is to be part of an education system. To do so, we need to see whether having had pre-school experience in a free play setting does indeed enhance children's cognitive, social and emotional development.

The need for pre-school provision

In one sense, all children receive a pre-school 'education' just by being alive, by seeing, hearing, smelling and so forth what their bodies can do and what goes on around them – the very earliest stages, perhaps, of 'the school of life'. This fact – that even the very youngest babies experience all sorts of sensations and observe all sorts of happenings and gradually absorb from them a tremendous amount of knowledge of their world – could be supplemented by an idea that has been very powerful in our understanding of children's learning (an idea we will discuss in Chapter 4) – that young children can learn effectively only through their own spontaneous investigations of their environment, that the only motivation operating is their need to solve their own individual, internally arising, self-posed, and immediately pressing problems, and if we impose or induce any other motivation, such as seeking to please the teacher or win her praise, we will disturb the child's 'natural' way of learning.

There are very complex and difficult issues here about what children are like and what 'education' is, which we tease out in Chapter 4; for the moment we will just point out that this argument could imply that there should be no special provision at all for the education of young children. The argument would be that children do learn from their day-to-day living, that they can only learn from that and there's no point teaching them (or even that teaching them interferes with their development), so just let them grow, without any more special attention or facilities than will preserve them from serious physical harm. People who believe in this argument might extend it to later stages of education too, abolishing all formal schooling; or they might, less radically, agree that older children do have to be taught, but maintain that young ones should not be, either because they have not yet become 'ready' to profit from instruction or to preserve their freedom and spontaneity for as long as possible. We go into the validity of some of these ideas later. However, a verdict on the idea of the child as being entirely an individualistic learner who is not taught or helped to learn by other people can clearly be given here. It just is not true. 'The child's environment' obviously includes other people and social institutions. Having to live with other people is indeed one source of the child's own 'internally arising' intellectual problems, and of their solutions. In fact some scientists concerned with why *homo sapiens* developed so much more brain and intelligence than other species argue that it was because early Man lived in social groups whose members had to be intelligent in order to get on with each other successfully. Whether this hypothesis is correct or not, it is clear that all societies make some sort of social provision for even the earliest stages of children's education and it is extremely unusual for the child to be left alone and never taught at all: the only questions to be asked are 'who provides the education?', 'when?', and 'what sort of education should it be?'.

One traditional answer to the question 'who should provide the child's education?' is 'the family'. Families do indeed educate their children and the most accurate single predictor of a child's educational attainment is still that of his or her parents. Nevertheless, it has long been recognised that the family should not be the only educator of the child, and schools are provided, in fact are compulsory, for all children between 5 and 16. A few children do not go to school because their parents satisfy the state that they can provide the children with a good education outside the school system, but they are very much the exception. State and parents normally agree that it is a good thing, both for the individual child and for the wider society, that all children except the most severely mentally and physically handicapped should go to school. There may be less agreement on *why* it is a good thing and about what schooling should consist of, but the need to educate children and the good sense of not leaving this entirely to their families are seen as obvious.

Does this apply to the years before school attendance is compulsory? Should there be 'schools' for 'pre-school' children, or can their education be left to their families? Here there is still real disagreement, and coming to a sensible answer involves many considerations. Among them are the characteristics, needs and competences of young children; the characteristics, needs and competences of their families; the characteristics of 'pre-school schools'; the similarities and differences among the effects on children and families of different existing ways of providing children with pre-school education; what we would hope early childhood education could be. We do not have space to consider all these fully, and in any case there are many serious gaps in the information available. We will therefore deal very briefly indeed with some of these points, spending most time here on reviewing the effectiveness of pre-school education, where new evidence has recently become available.

There seems to us to be little doubt that since the Second World War there has been rather too heavy an emphasis in both theory and policy on family life (mainly life with Mum) being the only fit place for all under-fives. We do not deny that mother–child relationships are important for the child's development (and for the mother's; see below), but it is clear that young children, even babies, *normally* and *naturally* form relationships with other people who make important contributions to the child's life. Relating *exclusively* to Mum can be disadvantageous in at least three ways: first it means you have no substitute relationship if Mum has to go away or cannot provide what you need; second you cannot so easily learn things she cannot teach you, such as how to have characteristics or skills she herself hasn't got or how to manage two or more relationships at once; third, it places pretty high demands on Mum, a point we will return to later. Michael Rutter, reviewing all the evidence in *Maternal Deprivation Reassessed* (1981), concludes that what is best is a warm and consistent relationship with not just Mum but *several* people who know and are concerned for the child, so that they can stand in for each other should one have to be absent, and can make complementary contributions to the child's well-being and education. From before their first birthday, and increasingly thereafter, children can have differentiated relationships with different people, preferring this one as a source of comfort in distress, that one as an exciting person to play with. Something much more like an extended family, where half a dozen people are deeply and consistently committed to the children's development and share its responsibilities – that is, are social 'parents' – seems to be the most comfortable situation for young children to grow up in vis-à-vis adults. It is worth pointing out that it is also probably satisfactory for the child to spend some time tête-a-tête with these 'parents' and some time in a less intimate social group where more people are involved, though still not very large numbers, and with stable and caring adults in charge. This is the sort of dual experience that kibbutz children have, and children in the good-quality daycare institutions described by Alison Clarke-Stewart (1982).

A group containing a few adults and several children will also allow many opportunities for relationships between children. Until recently we have underestimated young children's capacity for peer relationships, perhaps because of focusing too much on the mother–child dyad. It is now clear that, from babyhood onwards, children show an interest in children near to them in age that is different from the interest they show in adults, seeking to play with peers, and if they are familiar showing a great deal of understanding of them. Judy Dunn's study of siblings in Cambridge families shows this particularly well (Dunn, 1984), and many studies of pre-school groups have reported that children who see each other at playgroup or nursery become friends and playmates, able to use their knowledge of other children to get along with them, to share things, to please their peers or annoy them, to co-operate in role play or construction games or rough-and-tumble. The social importance of peers, like the benefits of close and friendly relationships with several adults, suggests that young children should not be confined to a one-to-one relationship with Mum.

But are there limits on what sort and amount of social interaction are beneficial? Yes: young children get on less well if they meet unpredictably changing care from adults who replace each other on too rapid a schedule. This is bad partly because it involves too much breaking of relationships, an experience that nobody, child or adult, finds pleasant, and that young children have particular trouble coping with because they do not know either why there is, all of a sudden, a new adult to care for them, or that the old caretaker will be back next week to pick up the relationship where it was left off and still cares *about* them even though temporarily absent. It is bad also because, if there are many caretakers, each knows the child less well, and the child also knows less about each caretaker. Since young children are still novices at talking and communication they are immediately at a practical disadvantage if they have to make their needs, wishes and interests known to someone who does not know about the idiosyncracies of their attempts to communicate. Adults who know a child well can often make out what he or she means almost before it is said – indeed the child may have the impression that adults are omniscient precisely because they are so often able to discover things from the child's most inadequate utterances or gestures, indeed to discover things the child would have preferred to hide! Adults who are unfamiliar with the child will find whatever he or she says less intelligible – and if they do not have shared knowledge they will be less able to respond appropriately to what is said even if it is intelligible.

We know from recent studies of language development that the optimum experience for good and rapid development contains a fairly high rate of the child's utterances being reacted to by adults who acknowledge, extend and act on what is said in ways that pick up the child's intentions as well as the child's meaning – 'child-contingent dialogue'. Children who have caretakers who cannot do this because they do not know enough about the individual child will therefore be having a sub-optimum experience for development. There may well be analogies to be drawn about what is the optimum experience for cognitive development more generally: child-contingent co-operation between adult and child, including dialogue, is probably a contributor to children's ability to concentrate, to persevere despite difficulties and to see the significance of what they are doing (though we are a bit ahead of the evidence here). In short, children profit from having shared experience with their caretakers, and from discussing it with them. Again, this does not mean that they should live entirely within the family, although the family can indeed supply them with adults who have the familiarity that child-contingent dialogue requires. However, it does mean that pre-school experience should be – most of the time – provided in fairly small groups so the participants can know each other as individuals with shared experience and joint activities.

Looked at from what we know of young children's characteristics, needs and competences, then, it seems that spending some of their time outside the family might be quite a good thing for young children because it extends their experience with adults and with peers, and provides experience of being in a larger social group than the family. It may also provide experiences with materials that don't fit very easily into many family environments: climbing frames, sandpits, finger paints and so forth need more domestic space and resources than many families have.

Is provision for pre-school children outside the family also a good thing for the family? It would appear that parents believe it is, since the overwhelming majority say they want it for their children, and in fact most children in Britain at present do go to some sort of pre-school group before starting school. When asked why they want it, the most frequent answers parents give are concerned with preparing the child for school and helping him or her to get on with other children: reasonable things to want for your child. (We will see whether there is evidence that pre-school experience provides them later.) The amount of pre-school provision that parents want varies: few want much in the way of pre-school groups for their babies, but most want it for their 4 year olds. On the whole, parents want there to be pre-school provision available for their child and to be able to choose when he or she attends – both the age of beginning and the number of hours. There is, however, a massive gap between demand, which is high, and number of available places, which is low. Some parents need pre-school provision for practical reasons: quite a high proportion of mothers of pre-school children are in employment and need caretakers for the children. Despite what some reactionary politicians say, we would not reduce problems if we removed mothers of pre-school children from the labour market since most are working because they need the money and at pay rates that would be too low to be attractive to most men. Even more importantly, it is very clear that confining mothers to the company of their pre-school children without adequate social and financial support puts them at risk of severe and longlasting depression, and this in turn makes it less likely that their children will enjoy the sort of interaction we know to be optimal for their development. The provision of more facilities for pre-school children would be of benefit not just to them but to the adults in the family responsible for them. We need good pre-school provision both for the children's sake and for their families' sake.

If we were designing pre-school provision from what we know about the characteristics of young children, we would make sure that all children had warm and stable relationships with caring adults, some of them very intimate and others more distant though still friendly and with mutual knowledge. These relationships with adults would involve a lot of interactions with joint activity, discussion of shared experience, and child-contingent dialogue. They would also involve the more experienced partner, the adult, 'scaffolding' the child's way through the performance and acquisition of complex skills: modelling them, supporting and extending the child's efforts, giving appropriate feedback and encouragement, providing opportunities for practice, motivating the child where effort is necessary, showing how the skill is useful or a desired part of the process of growing up in a culture. Our provision would make sure that children had opportunities to interact with other children, so that they could learn the social skills which are used between peers and begin to move out from the family into the social world of childhood. Given that, beginning at the age of 5, children are by law obliged to spend something like 15,000 hours in schools, we might be wise to prepare children for that experience too. We would not separate children from their families or the familiar world but would supplement them with an introduction to the world of formal learning. Pre-school education that approximates to these requirements has existed – if not in sufficient quantity – for some time. Can we say anything about its effects?

The effectiveness of pre-school education

There have been many studies of whether pre-school experience gives children an advantage that benefits them through the rest of their childhood. Some studies used IQ scores as a measure of this advantage, others have looked at various measures of social behaviour. Much of the research was done during the 1960s, when providing special pre-school education was regarded as a way of reducing the effects of poverty, deprivation and disadvantage. The American 'Head Start' programme, for example, was based on the idea that adding a lump of good educational experience to the early lives of poor children would act like a vaccination programme, giving them an initial advantage or inoculating them against later problems so that they would show less of the underachievement and alienation from school and society that are common and handicapping in the most disadvantaged social groups. Thinking of pre-school experience in this way now seems unsatisfactory: it implies that there is little that is good in the experience of young children outside the pre-school programme or in the culture of the so-called disadvantaged groups, and it overlooks the importance of later experiences in the wider social and economic structures that have to do with social inequalities. Nevertheless, the research is worth looking at briefly because we can glean from it some indications of whether pre-school experience affects children in the short term and in the long term, and of which sorts of pre-school provision have which effects. Research that looks at the detail of *how* effects come about and that relates this to accounts of how young children learn will be discussed later.

The short-term result of the Head Start programme and of similar interventions in other countries was that children from severely disadvantaged backgrounds who had gone through pre-school intervention programmes showed higher IQ scores in their first year of primary school than did children who had not. They also made a more favourable impression on their teachers, and tended to do better at early reading and arithmetic. However, in most studies the differences between graduates of pre-school programmes and children from similar backgrounds who had not been to pre-school became smaller as the children got older, so that in the early 1970s some researchers and policymakers concluded that pre-school provision could not raise the later performance of children who came from educationally underachieving social groups, and could not be an effective way of reducing social disadvantage and inequality. Its short-term effects were said to 'wash out': IQ went up fast then drifted back down, and though children were initially doing better in school they were not in the end ahead in the educational race. Barbara Tizard concluded, for example, 'In so far, then, as the expansion of early schooling is seen as a way of avoiding later school failure or of closing the social class gap in achievement, we already know it to be doomed to failure ... pre-school education has no long-term effect on later school achievement' (Tizard, 1975). Jensen (1969) said, in so many words, 'compensatory education has been tried, and it has failed.'

Recently, however, evidence has emerged from the American research that suggests a more optimistic conclusion about special pre-school intervention programmes. The Consortium for Longitudinal Studies set up a collaboration between researchers which combined and evaluated the results of the best-designed and best-documented Head Start programmes. It followed up children who had taken part in these programmes when they were young adults. Altogether, about 2,000 'programme graduates' and 'controls' were traced, almost all of them Black and from low-income families. As well as IQ and achievement scores, data on their school careers, their self-concepts and their out-of-school experience were collected. The results from the different studies are reasonably consistent (Woodhead, 1983). The 'graduates' have not maintained the IQ gain that showed up for the first two years of their ordinary schooling, and they are only slightly better than 'controls' at school reading and mathematics. However, their actual school careers differed significantly from those of the controls. They were much less likely to be moved out of mainstream education into special education and they were less likely to have been made to repeat a grade (year) in school or to have left school before completing the high school course. As the pre-school graduates were *not* doing much better in school, so far as objective tests were concerned, what had changed was what was done for children who were doing rather badly in the ordinary classroom. Children who were not pre-school graduates were likely to be taken out of the mainstream class when they didn't cope with it well, and to be put in special classes which had special educational programmes, and no doubt everyone expected less of them. Similarly they were more likely to be kept down to repeat a grade while their agemates went on to the next grade. Pre-school graduates were more likely to receive remedial help while remaining in the ordinary class with their peers. Thus they were less likely to be prominently labelled as failures, less likely to be seen by themselves and by others as 'people who will not get on well in the school system'.

This showed up in the interview data that the Consortium researchers collected. When they were asked to tell the interviewer about something that had made them feel proud of themselves, the pre-school graduates were more likely to mention school or work achievements, while the control group mentioned *morally* praiseworthy acts, or said, sadly, that nothing had ever made them feel proud of themselves. We may not like this emphasis on achievement and competition, but lack of achievement motivation may be a factor in lack of school success.

In one of the Consortium studies, the Perry Preschool Project (which is still continuing as the High/Scope Program), there were other significant differences in social outcomes (Weikart *et al.*, 1978). The graduates, having been rated as somewhat better adjusted in school, had committed fewer delinquent acts, were less likely to face criminal charges arising from their minor crimes and misdemeanours, were less likely to be chronic offenders, and, in the case of the girls, were less likely to become a teenage mother. This sort of evidence suggests that the pre-school programme experience *was* effective in removing severe disadvantages, and that it *may* open up life chances that might not otherwise be available. It did not, however, lead to its graduates becoming just like high-achieving middle-class children, so Barbara Tizard's pessimistic conclusion is merely shaken, not knocked down.

Because the main effects seemed to come about through changes in the way schools handled 'failing' children, because the children who participated in the programmes were Black with initially low IQs and from families suffering severe socio-economic disadvantage, and because the pre-school programmes were somewhat unusual (high teacher–child ratio, enthusiastic implementation of specially designed programmes – but also brief), we cannot be certain that the positive effects found by the Consortium can be generalised to other settings. They are, however, in some ways interestingly similar to the results of a French study of adoption carried out by Michel Schiff and his colleagues (1986). This study traced a sample of thirty-two children adopted within the first month of life into upper-middle-class families. Their biological mothers and the putative fathers were all unskilled workers, some of them very obviously social and intellectual failures. The children's IQ scores and school careers were compared with those of school children of the general population and of the two contrasting social classes, and with a child of their biological mother who was near in age. These siblings or half siblings had not been adopted into middle-class families; instead they were being reared in unskilled workers' families, mostly with their biological mother though some were with grandparents or a foster mother. The results were quite clear. Although the adopted children and their non-adopted siblings had at least one parent in common and sometimes two, their IQs and school careers were quite different. Each resembled the average of their social class of rearing, so the adopted children with their middle-class experience had high average IQs and very few scored below the normal range, and few were in remedial classes, let alone in permanent special education. Of their non-adopted siblings, brought up in a milieu of unskilled workers, two-thirds were in remedial classes, half of these in permanent special education, and more than one in five had an IQ below 85. Here, too, differences in experience seemed to be associated with some difference on test scores and a marked difference in how schools handled a child's 'failure'.

Two studies of large samples going through ordinary pre-schools in England and Wales have recently been published. The smaller sample was studied by researchers concerned with the National Survey of Health and Development (Wadsworth, 1986). This study began with a sample of several thousand born in 1946 and has recently included investigations of the first-born children of these people, the Second Generation. About 1,600 children from the Second Generation were tested at the age of 8. Children with pre-school experience gained somewhat higher scores on vocabulary, reading and sentence completion tests than children without pre-school education. Whether children had had pre-school experience made more difference to their scores three years later than how much stimulation they had had at home, though less difference than the most important predictor of their ability, which was their mother's education. These findings suggest that, for this generation, going to a nursery school, class or playgroup makes a positive contribution to verbal abilities. The rise is not large, but it is there.

The second set of results comes from researchers concerned with the Child Health and Education Study (CHES), which is a longitudinal survey of all the children born in one week of April 1970 (Osborn and Milbank, 1987). Assessments of these children at the ages of 5 and 10 have been used to examine the effectiveness of their pre-school experience: more than 5,000 children who attended nursery schools or classes, day nurseries or playgroups have been compared with nearly 4,000 who did not. Making this comparison was complicated by the variation that exists in what sort of pre-school places are available to parents: depending on where they live there may or may not be local authority nursery schools or classes, and these may or may not have long waiting lists and restrictions on provision. When families have unequal access to pre-school provision, we cannot believe that the children entering one sort of pre-school are equivalent to those entering another sort or to those staying at home. So, if we find differences between children graduating from different sorts of pre-school or not attending any pre-school, we cannot confidently attribute them to the effects of the pre-school experience. We know too little about what characteristics of families make them more or less good for their children's development to be able to identify everything we must allow for to distinguish pre-school's effects from home experience's. However, the Child Health and Education Study has carefully made statistical allowances for a large number of 'intervening variables', such as social status, type of family and various characteristics of the mother, that might affect both the children's test scores and the sort of pre-school experience they have. Similar allowances were made for aspects of the children's experience between 5 and 10 years of age, such as the social mobility of the family upwards or downwards and the type of primary school attended.

The outcome of careful analyses was that children who had pre-school experience scored significantly higher on a number of tests at 5 and at 10 than did children who had no pre-school experience. Whether or not you had been to nursery class or school, day nursery or playgroup made more difference to your score than your gender, your family size or how much interest your parents took in your education, though the 'intervening variable' that made most difference was the Social Index measure of socio-economic inequality. That is, pre-school experience raised the scores of both advantaged and disadvantaged children – not an enormous amount, but reliably – both immediately afterwards and at the end of primary schooling. Although the most socially disadvantaged children gained slightly more from their pre-school experience, there was a general benefit for all children, so that social inequalities in cognitive test performance were not much reduced. In this sample there were no clear associations between pre-school experience and social behaviour or personality measures, apart from a possible finding that children who attended local authority nursery classes or day nurseries were a bit more overactive and extrovert.

A final point from this study concerns the children who did not have any sort of pre-school experience. They mostly came from the most disadvantaged part of the population, from families where there were poor housing conditions, low income, insecure employment and other stresses. These disadvantages would have made it harder for parents to find pre-school provision for their children and also to provide an optimum home environment for them. The children are thus doubly disadvantaged during their pre-school years; and, given the evidence for long-term effects that the recent American and British research presents, their disadvantage is likely to persist through their school careers. The Head Start programmes involved severely disadvantaged children – poor, Black, low IQ and with under-educated mothers. It might be argued that the programmes produced a significant effect on these children simply because they were so disadvantaged that any intervention would raise their scores, and that no improvement would be shown for less disadvantaged children. Thus we might 'rescue' the bottom level of children but it would be of little use to provide pre-school education for any but the most disadvantaged. The British studies that we have discussed, and the American data, suggest that, on the contrary, *all* children benefited from the programmes, though possibly the most disadvantaged children, with most ground to make up, did gain somewhat more than their more advantaged peers. If we do want to reduce disadvantage and educational inequality, the provision of high-quality pre-school education and care has a worthwhile contribution to make, in that as well as benefiting all children it may be particularly helpful to the most disadvantaged, to those who are most likely not to benefit from later schooling.

This consistent pattern of short-term IQ gains from pre-school experience that 'wash out', plus a continuing effect on children's ability to cope with the basic demands of schooling, does not fit the 'inoculation against failure' model very well. As we and many others have said, this model overlooks the importance of other experiences in the wider social and economic structures that have to do with social inequalities. Many influences on the family and the school modify the effects of pre-school experience on children's attitudes and achievements and are in turn modified by them. It now seems that while the pre-school may have taught children some concrete cognitive skills and content – shape, colour, number, etc. – it also, perhaps more importantly, exposed them to other cognitive skills of more pervasive relevance to school. They learned to concentrate, to follow instructions, to persevere, to make a good impression on their teachers, to enjoy school activities. Pre-school graduates had positive attitudes to school and its classroom activities, were able to cope with the social demands of the classroom, and were able to learn and to feel competent. Their teachers would see their competence and, expecting them to continue to do well, would encourage success and regard failure as a temporary matter to be remediated in the classroom. A child who has not acquired these basic cognitive skills would have to learn them in the hurly-burly of the classroom, and appearing to himself and to those around him as less competent might have and elicit lower expectations about his achievement. A 'transactional' model such as this might account for the research results better than claiming that 'inoculation against failure' temporarily raised the IQ and then had separate longer-term effects on cognition.

Characteristics of successful pre-school programmes

Is it the case that different forms of pre-school provision have different effects? Might some be more effective than others? Should parents be involved? What should be in the curriculum? How important is the professional training of the staff? Should provision be of schools, of nurseries, of playgroups, of support to parents? When should children go into a pre-school programme and how much time should they spend there? Are playgroups more likely to foster creativity, nursery schools better literacy, day nurseries peer group social skills? There is wide debate over questions like these. Because the intake for different programmes varies it is very hard to answer such questions. The research data certainly do not suggest that there is an obvious candidate for the status of 'best pre-school provision', and as both children and desirable effects vary perhaps we should not expect one. However, certain characteristics of successful programmes may be inferred from the literature.

All the Consortium studies with positive effects had a high level of professional support and a low ratio of children to staff, that is, the children involved probably enjoyed a good access to individual attention from an adult. British pre-schools do not usually enjoy as low a ratio as the Consortium projects (5:1), though this is typical of day nurseries, but it is worth noting that in the CHES study the local authority nursery classes, which often had a child–adult ratio of greater than 10:1, produced less improvement in children's achievement than other forms of pre-school provision. CHES's findings showed that playgroups, day nurseries and nursery schools all had beneficial effects, which were of similar magnitude once various social factors in the children and their families had been taken into account. They suggest that 'provided the child receives proper care, had interesting activities and other children to play with . . . the actual type of pre-school experience matters little' (Osborn and Milbank, 1987, p. 239).

The CHES study did not, however, match variation in the 'curricular' experience provided by pre-school with outcomes for the children in any exhaustive way. Their results did show that pre-school's effects on children were enhanced if the mothers were themselves involved in the pre-school, which the Consortium's results also, though less conclusively, suggested. As well as the opportunities for especially affectionate teaching that this no doubt offered the child, being involved in their children's pre-school activities may have raised mothers' aspirations for their children and supported their child-rearing activities. Further, the presence of mothers will have reduced child:adult ratios. Beyond this documented effect, we know rather little about the effectiveness of different pre-school curricula. One of the issues that needs discussing is by what means programmes have their effect. Is it better to seek to teach a few 'crucial' and specific cognitive skills such as answering questions? Or to teach the whole range of cognitive skills, which will contribute to later schooling? Or to motivate children to develop these skills themselves? Or to encourage children to believe in the possibility of finding school an arena for their success and enjoyment?

In this debate over whether we should teach for specific cognitive goals or for more pervasive attitudinal ones there are relevant theoretical perspectives (which we discuss in Chapter 4) but, as yet, little conclusive evidence on which approaches are most effective or most enjoyable. As even teaching some highly specific cognitive skill might enhance the child's general sense of competence and would probably involve other generalisable cognitive skills (such as attending to a teacher, remembering, etc.), it may be hard to get clear-cut differences between approaches.

One aspect of development that has come up in the research studies already discussed has been the effect of pre-school experience on children's sense of competence. Part of the rationale for free play was that setting their goals and achieving them through their own efforts would enhance children's belief in their own ability to do things and hence their willingness to take on tasks and persist with them despite difficulties. Being able to behave like this will be very advantageous in school, where work becomes increasingly individualised and in the later stages is also competitive. It is also probably an important component of successful coping with all sorts of life stresses. It seems possible that some people who are seriously disadvantaged do limit their opportunities even further by assuming they will fail when objectively they would have a fair hope of succeeding, or by making choices that are certain to increase their disadvantages when alternative choices might have improved their position. Some of the American studies of special pre-school intervention programmes suggest that they may have worked by giving the participating children and their parents more positive expectations of the children's potential. They made the children more able to cope independently with the demands of school. This, plus the small increase in cognitive and linguistic skills we have already discussed, made a more favourable impression on teachers, and a 'virtuous cycle' of better performance, higher expectation and better teaching was set up. It could not be said that the American studies provide strong evidence for this course of events, and the British studies discussed do not give us any supporting evidence. The CHES data include some measures of self-concept at 10, but these are not different for graduates of pre-school and non-attenders.

An observational study by Sandra Jowett and Kathy Sylva focused on the cognitive challenge of pre-school activities. Ninety working-class children who had attended either local authority nursery schools or local playgroups were observed in the reception class of their infant schools. When nursery graduates were engaged in play in the reception class at the end of their first term, they were significantly more likely to be purposefully or creatively engaged: 75 per cent of their activity was of high cognitive challenge. They also gave more attention to formal 'educational' tasks such as reading, doing workcards and writing. They spent less time just passively watching other children, though nursery and playgroup graduates did not differ in their social part-icipation. While sustained conversations were rare, nursery graduates more often had such dialogue with peers, and were somewhat more likely to offer suggestions and questions. They made more social and 'learning-oriented' remarks to the teacher and seemed less passively dependent on her. When they met a problem they were more likely to persevere with attempts to solve it themselves and less likely give up or ask for help. Thus they seemed more autonomous and more 'ready' for the demands of school. This suggests that different pre-school regimes may affect competence differently, at least as far as working-class children are concerned. Children who had attended nursery schools with a relatively demanding and structured curriculum were doing better as self-running learners in the reception class of infant school than their peers who had been to playgroups offering unstructured free play. Some obligation on children to be competent planners and completers of activities – as in the structured interventions of Head Start – may be an important component of pre-school experience.

Finally, one benefit that was claimed for pre-school provision during the period when it was being proposed as a panacea for educational inequality was that it would improve children's language development. This proposal rested on a belief that some children had a severely impoverished home language environment and came to school without enough language competence to cope with its demands. We have seen that attending pre-school does make a small positive difference to language use, but it is also now known that many children whose language in school is indeed inadequate are in fact very competent language users at home. We will also see in the next chapter that there is little to be complacent about in what use is made of language in pre-school settings, or indeed in the infant classes that follow them. Too many children seem to be incompetent language users at school but use language fluently and effectively at home.

If we look back on 'the effectiveness of pre-school education' we see that there were high hopes which turned out to be unrealistic. This disappointment led policymakers to dismiss pre-school as a worthwhile way of improving educational performance. Recently we have begun to find evidence that going to pre-school does produce an improvement in children's cognition and language, though it is a small one and in some studies it decreases over time. There is also evidence that going to pre-school changes children's attitudes to learning for the better, and raises their parents' and teachers' hopes for their achievement and the support they give the child's learning. If all these effects can be made to occur together, and to a larger extent than they do at present, and if the later school experience that children meet can 'follow through' and keep them going, then pre-school education would be very effective and very worthwhile indeed. In the rest of this book we examine how the present effect comes about, what psychological theory has to offer, and two ways the curriculum might be supplemented to enhance the effectiveness of pre-school.

CHAPTER 3

The Details of Teaching and Learning as Seen in Pre-school

We can provide a highly detailed picture of what teachers and children do (and *don't* do) in nursery schools and classes and in playgroups because there has been a great deal of relevant research in the last ten years or so. Teachers and 3–5 year olds have been observed in London, Stoke-on-Trent, Cambridge, Oxfordshire, Sheffield, Bristol, and elsewhere. The different studies have had different aims and different methods, but they do in the end provide much the same account of what was happening and what was good and bad about it. We are going to begin our account by describing how one of these studies was done, so that readers can get a feel of the methods used to produce a picture of early childhood education that is similar to all the other researchers' pictures but rather different from what the free play enthusiasts thought was going on.

The Open University study of teaching styles in nursery education

The Open University study (Meadows and Cashdan, 1983) was one of the large-scale studies commissioned by the Social Science Research Council in the mid-1970s. Its aims were to characterise the range and variation in teaching style and child behaviour in a group of teachers and their classes in typical mainstream nursery schools over a period of four school terms, and to investigate the effects of a special experimental teaching programme implemented in the classroom. We were concerned with both behaviour and attitude: did teachers with different views on children and on education differ in their behaviour, and what could we find out about the *children's* attitudes to teachers and to themselves as learners. The researchers (Sara Meadows, Asher

Cashdan, Janet Philps, Ronny Flynn and Jenny Weaver) worked with twenty teachers in nursery schools in Outer London boroughs, making detailed observations of how teachers and children behaved throughout the nursery class session and of how the teacher worked alone with one child at a time in a short lesson specially set up for the research project. The teachers were all interviewed about their views of the children in the class, and half of them took part in a special teaching intervention, which is described in Chapter 5. Here we will concentrate on how the observations were made and what they told us about the educational climate of the nursery school.

We wanted to get a systematic, representative picture of what teachers and children said and did, moment by moment, during the ordinary school day. This meant that we could not rely on anecdotes or on sitting in a classroom getting a general idea of what went on. We wanted to be able to say exactly how often one thing or another happened, what led most often to this and less often to that, what sort of person approached what sort of activity in what sort of way. These are facts that can be discovered only by making detailed records of behaviour, second by second, and then carefully analysing them. Filmed records of behaviour would have allowed us to check exactly what happened more than pen and paper records could, but they are expensive and very time-consuming to analyse, and the presence of a camera in a classroom tends to disrupt what people would normally do more than the presence of a human observer unobtrusively scribbling away. Having a visiting adult in the classroom is familiar enough in most schools not to cause much of a disturbance except at the very beginning of the visit.

So we chose, like others of the 1970s researchers, to have a trained observer unobtrusively present in the classroom filling in a detailed record of what went on. We recorded the teacher–child interaction from the teacher's end and from the child's. For three minutes at a time we noted down what teacher or child did and said to whom, and with what consequences, according to lists of sorts of behaviour (for example, 'suggestion by teacher', 'teacher repeats or acknowledges child's remark', 'dealing with play equipment', 'administration', 'child's use of materials', 'child's distance from adult') which we had worked out in exploratory studies. Three minutes is a short time but in practice it was as long as we could manage to keep up an accurate record of either teacher's or child's side of an interaction plus an out-line of other participants' behaviour! We took about forty observa-tions of each of our twenty teachers spread across their time with pupils but making more observations during the free play part of the day than during storytime or milk sessions: for each of eight children in each teacher's group we took at least four observations of that child during free play. We took observations like this in the first and third terms of one school year, and the first term of the next year. In the end this amounted to about forty hours of teachers' activity and twenty hours of children's, including more than 36,000 teacher utterances, and more than 2,800 bouts of children's play. Quite a large sample.

What teachers do in nursery classes

If we look at what our observations of teachers tell us about what they were doing, we find they were busy almost all the time and that most of this busy-ness was to do with children. We classified teachers' behaviour into the following categories:

'administration', including formal discussions and meetings, planning the day, marking the register, attending to parents and visitors, writing records, etc.;

'housework', which included cleaning, opening and shutting windows, setting dinner tables, and general tidying up, though *not* anything that involved play equipment;

'dealing with play equipment', for example preparing, fixing, mending, putting away and providing it;

'physical child care', such as helping with buttons, wiping noses, toileting, serving lunch, and so forth;

'minimal supervision', with no interaction with the children or other activity (beyond perhaps 'recharging the batteries'!);

'play', that is, being engaged in the play activity itself rather than supervising it or helping the child to do it;

'affection and comfort';

'listening and watching only';

'non-verbal group activity', such as dancing, miming, organising group games;

'demonstrating', either a skill or the use of materials;

'helping', for example steadying a piece of paper while the child cuts it with scissors;

'investigating/examining' objects (or people);

'showing', that is, pointing or offering something for the purpose of drawing the child's attention to it rather than offering it for play or other purposes.

Teachers' language was also categorised. The main categories here were as follows:

'directions' – the 'do this' or 'don't do that', with or without explanations, including general requests, reprimands and so forth;

'general remarks' – the social oil of conversation, such as greetings, requests for remarks to be repeated, jokes;

'positive comments' – more focused remarks of encouragement, assent, humouring, enthusiasm, reassurance and praise;

'singing, reciting and reading';

'information' – giving or seeking simple or complex information;

'suggestions', such as 'would you like to have a story?', or 'you could make a runway for that aeroplane now' (provided that it was a genuine suggestion that the child might go along with or not, rather than a politely phrased command!);

'instruction' – a 'how to' verbalisation involving fairly specific statements; and

'draws attention' – remarks like 'look', 'have you seen?', 'did you hear the cuckoo clock?' and so forth.

Finally, teachers' behaviour was coded according to the cognitive demands it made on the children, and also in terms of whether it was associated with a follow-up of an action by a child. We distinguished between:

'minimal cognitive demands', which only required the child to observe or to answer at most 'yes' or 'no', or involved inexplicit directions or suggestions such as 'why don't you do something else?';

'simple cognitive demands', where the child received simple direction or was asked a question requiring a one- or two-word answer given with little thought, such as 'what colour are your shoes?'; and

'complex cognitive demands', which included everything more demanding than this – though not all these would look 'complex' to people outside the nursery child's world!

Teachers spent only 2 per cent of their time on 'minimal supervision', 4 per cent on administration and 10 per cent on housework. 'Minimal supervision' meant no visible activity, certainly no interaction with children, but both administration and housework sometimes involved children, as they included taking the register and clearing up, in which children took part. Teachers frequently talked to children, but rarely did they play with them, demonstrate things to them, help them or investigate things with them – none of these categories came to more than 3 per cent. In all, the teacher was to some extent involved in the child's activity as tutor about 15 per cent of the time. When we looked at what was said, nearly 60 per cent of the teachers' remarks made no cognitive demand at all, not even asking for a simple action or an answer to a simple yes/no question, and most remarks were 'one-offs' where the teacher said something, the child might answer but wasn't particularly expected to, and the teacher nearly always did not follow up any response the child made. Teachers initiated 60 per cent of their utterances, and only a little more than 10 per cent of their remarks followed up a child's response. More than 20 per cent of teachers' remarks were entirely social – positive comments such as 'that's a nice picture', general social formulae such as 'hello', and repetitions or acknowledgements of a remark by the child. Another 30 per cent were simple questions or simple statements – 'what colour is this pencil?', 'are you hot?', 'that's a submarine', 'I like balloons'. Only about 10 per cent of teachers' remarks were at all complex, and only 4 per cent required the child to do anything as complex as produce a sentence of more than two words, remember something, or answer a 'why' or 'how' question. This was the picture during the free play sessions, which made up the major part of the day. We also observed the teachers during milk, music, story and clearing-up periods. As might be expected, their behaviour differed in some ways during these observations. Story and music sessions had more complex fact statement, stories had more questions and more drawing attention, while music had many instructions. All these sessions had more directions – both 'do this' and 'don't do that' – than free play time.

We interviewed the teachers to find out about their views of the children in their classes, both because we wanted to discover what concepts they used in thinking about children and because, in the shorter term, we wanted to observe in detail children who they saw as functioning well or poorly in the nursery school. Their concepts were too rich and varied to describe here, but two aspects are worth noting. First, all the teachers used concepts that went together to describe the 'well-functioning' or 'poorly functioning' child, mentioning things like 'can't concentrate', 'a really bright child', 'good at everything', 'not very interested in school things', and so forth. Second, despite the researchers' encouragement to do so, they did *not* use terms referring to developmental changes in the child or to the child's relations with the teacher. This might suggest they saw the children in rather static, uninfluenceable, impersonal terms.

These results suggested to us that these teachers were busy, sensitive and nice to the children, but not really very demanding. Having provided materials, they were contributing to keeping the classroom running smoothly. They did not get involved in activities themselves at all often, and they have very brief, undemanding chats with children rather than serious conversations. We will see what the children were up to later.

Our findings do not stand alone. A number of other research projects investigated staff behaviour in nursery schools and other pre-school groups. A team from the National Foundation for Educational Research (NFER) looked at the aims, role and deployment of staff in the nursery (Clift, 1980). They visited nine schools, twenty-six classes with a single teacher and five classes with more than one teacher, and worked with one teacher and one assistant in each. A total of 2,135 children attended these nurseries, mostly part time. The staff were interviewed about their aims and their role, and they were observed during a morning and an afternoon session.

The largest proportion of their time, over 40 per cent, was spent involved in children's activity, a further fifth was spent supervising the children, and about 15 per cent was taken up with chatting to the children, watching them and attending to their welfare. A fairly high proportion of time was spent organising equipment. More than 80 per cent of these activities were initiated by the staff themselves, with only 17 per cent the direct result of a child's or another adult's demand for their attention. Their activities were, however, fragmented. The average time for being involved in a child's activity was 98 seconds, for a conversation with children 35 seconds, for working with children 52 seconds. On average, staff changed task about 175 times in a two and a half hour session – approximately 70 tasks per hour. Even though many tasks were very brief, no more than an interpolated instant in an activity that continued, necessarily there were many occasions when the thread of the discourse or the play was lost, and time had to be spent in recovering a sense of what was going on or checking what had been done or said: time that could itself be subject to further interruption. These figures for the duration of activities and the rate of tasks undertaken suggest that it was very rare for staff to be able to sustain a focus on any task for long. Very few conversations lasted more than 1 minute.

Barbara Tizard and Janet Philps observed fifty-one staff and 109 children in twelve London units with different educational philosophies (Tizard *et al.*, 1976b,c). Here they found similar results to the NFER team's. Nearly half the time, staff were talking with children. Dealing with play equipment and housework took up 25 per cent, and supervision almost as much time. Playing with children was only seen 4 per cent of the time. Again, staff were busily concerned with the children but were not involved in their activity beyond talking about it.

This involvement on a purely verbal level might, of course, be all that is needed. However, the detail of these studies on teachers' language suggests a more unsatisfactory pattern. General social remarks, praise and repetitions of what the child has just said are common in all these studies; intellectually demanding remarks and questions, or remarks that extend the child's utterance, are rarer, particularly in Tizard's study and in research carried out by the Open University team. In both, the pattern of turntaking is very unequal. Characteristically the children's side of the conversation consists of single brief utterances, more often answers to the teacher's questions than either questions or remarks generated by the children themselves. Talk was a bit richer than this in nursery schools in Tizard's sample, which had a special commitment to facilitating children's language development, but the talk remained one-sided and simple. It is worth noting briefly that, even though staff spend so much of their time talking, each individual child will be spoken to only infrequently, as there are ten or so children for each staff member. Having a sustained conversation with an adult may be very rare indeed.

Here it may be of interest to consider another study of Barbara Tizard's which looked at 4 year olds talking to mothers and to teachers (Tizard and Hughes, 1984). The study concentrated particularly on the amount of conversation, its form (duration, who contributed what, and so forth) and its context. Radio microphone recordings were made (as in Gordon Wells' study of language development, 1985) of thirty little girls at home with their mothers and in schools with their teachers. Middle-class and working-class families were compared because of the widespread belief that working-class children did less well in school because their language at home was deficient. In fact, the recordings showed very few social class differences, even in school, but marked differences in the frequency and the quality of conversations at home and at school. Conversations were more frequent and longer at home, the average length of a school conversation being about eight turns and of a home conversation more than sixteen turns. Home conversations were more likely to start with the adult seeking to give information or explanation, which was the main reason why children initiated conversations in both places. School conversations took play activity as their topic in the majority of cases, while home conversations were more often concerned with other activities and with past or future events. The longest conversations in both settings concerned books that the adult read aloud; these conversations were one and a half to four times as long as conversations about play activities. There was much more joint activity at home, both play activity and non-play. Conversations were longer in joint play and looking at books together than they were when there was no joint activity. Children asked few questions at school and many at home; questions arising from the child's curiosity were particularly rare for working-class children at school. Teachers had the longest turns, about fourteen words on average, mothers about seven words and children five or six; teachers also took the main part in sustaining conversation with a child, while mother and child were more equal partners. In short, conversations at school were rarer, briefer and less equally balanced than at home. Tizard suggests that their meaning was shallower and the children were less interested at school; this implies, she believes, that teacher–child conversations may not foster children's cognition as one would hope. 'Readiness to question, to comment on the other's remarks, to contribute one's own reflexions and experiences, depends on the relative status of the participants in the conversation and the degree of intimacy between them' (Tizard and Hughes, 1984, p.75).

This sort of assertion is supported by the research done by David Wood and his colleagues under the auspices of the Oxford Pre-school Research Group (Wood *et al.*, 1980). They made a detailed analysis of audiotapes recorded for the purpose of looking at adult–child conversation in the pre-school. They found that responsibility for initiating conversations and keeping them going lay mainly with the adult. Wood describes two common styles of having conversations. One is to 'float', to be responsive to all the conversational remarks of all the children whether or not they carried on the topic in hand, which made for disjointed and superficial 'conversations', often brief, often little more than a string of acknowledgements of each turn. At the other extreme, adults often adopted a 'programmatic' style of conversation, dominating it with questions to which the child gives monosyllabic answers. Generally children did answer adults' questions appropriately, but their answers were commonly brief; while they rarely ignored questions or changed the subject they seldom followed up their own answers with a further elaboration or a question to the adult. The more the adult asked questions, the less the children contributed to the dialogue. If the adult made more 'contributions' – comments on her own activities or preferences, links between the present and other occasions, and so forth – the more the children asked questions and made contributions of their own.

Adults' remarks could be categorised according to topic. On average 11 per cent were to do with management, 28 per cent with instruction, 7 per cent with conversation and 30 per cent with interpersonal rapport, but in each case the variation amongst adults was considerable. It became clear that the more the adult talked about management, to the exclusion of other things, the more the children approached her to solve management issues such as being told what to do next or negotiating turns or receiving help with shoelaces or play equipment. When adults managed to avoid being supervisors and managers they could have more creative conversations. Most talk was context bound, about the here and now of what the child was doing; talk about the past and future, and about the 'why' of events and people's actions, was comparatively rare. Discussion of rules and social mores was mainly related to solving disputes; talk about absent people was mainly about the child's family.

It seems to be the case, then, that teachers who are operating a 'supervised free play' regime do not interact with their children in stimulating ways, nor do they have sustained conversations; they do their educational work indirectly through providing stimulating materials rather than through teaching directly or playing themselves. In this they are true to the method of 'play way' – they are leaving the children free to stimulate themselves, to be creative and to learn at their own rate. If we look at what the children are actually getting up to, do they seem to be absorbed, stimulated and learning, as the free play recipe says they should?

What children do in nursery classes

In the Open University study we looked carefully at our 2,809 play bouts in terms of what happened in them and in terms of the quality of the play. The aspects of quality we looked at were what play was focused on, how involved the child was, what use he or she made of material, how complex the activity was, and what sort of social participation was involved. We also looked at whether the child talked to adults or other children or was addressed by them, and at approximately how long activities lasted. On some of these qualities play varied a great deal. For example, about 36 per cent of play bouts were definitely focused on finding something out or doing some particular act, but 30 per cent were vague, unfocused or desultory; 43 per cent were solitary, but 22 per cent involved talking socially with other children and 18 per cent actually involved co-operating with them in play; 20 per cent made no use of material at all, 29 per cent only partially realised the potential use of material, but 47 per cent made full use of it. However, some qualities were relatively consistent. There was very little social interaction with adults and very little talk between adult and child. Children very rarely made original or creative use of material; most of their play was a simple repetition of one or two activities, 31 per cent at the level of just patting sand with a spade or daubing paint on paper and a further 28 per cent, though a trifle more complex, still seemed unorganised, for example play with sand which mixed patting and sand digging but in no discernible order. The observations of children showed some systematic variations related to characteristics of the child or of the material being used. Older children showed a higher level of involvement in their play, and engaged in more complex sequential play. They were less likely to show unfocused or purposeless activity or to make little or inadequate use of the material. They were a bit less likely to play entirely alone and more likely to play co-operatively with both adults and other children. They were more involved with talk with other children (though talking with adults was no more common with them than it was for younger children) and they stayed longer with their activities. Thus they showed the greater maturity and competence that one would expect.

There were fewer sex differences in children's behaviour. Boys predominated in the use of bicycles and balls, and were more likely to wander about doing nothing in particular (perhaps waiting for their turn with the bikes to come up?). Girls predominated in art and craft activities, and in domestic helping of the teacher; they were more often closer to the teacher. Rough-and-tumble play and aggression were rare in these nurseries, but boys were much more often involved than girls. Children who the teacher thought were 'well-functioning' showed less unfocused play, were more involved in their play, and showed less repetitive unsequenced play. They also got on better with other children, being more likely to talk a lot and receive a lot of talk from their peers and to co-operate with them, often as the obvious leader of the group. They stayed with their activities longer and tended to stay nearer adults, though adults did not talk to them more than they did to the 'poorly functioning' children. Thus our observations bore out the teachers' views about their children's competence.

Our observations showed that there was considerable variation between individual children in their free play behaviour and their use of school resources, which in many cases was evident from the beginning of their nursery school careers. Given a free choice of activity, many children showed quite restricted ranges of free play behaviour, spending most of their time on one or two sorts of material or types of games, whereas some others sampled the whole range of materials provided. They varied also in the cognitive content of their play and in their involvement in the social group. Some children were profiting from their good use of school, but others were not exploiting its resources to the full. The children appeared to be quite involved in their play and making reasonable use of their materials, but much of what they did seemed very simple, definitely not stretching them and rarely involving them in working with or talking with other people, particularly not with adults. Life was pleasant enough for most children – fights, quarrels or upsets were rare – but so were discovery, achievement after endeavour, and intellectual challenge. Some play bouts were brief and desultory, some went on interminably at the same repetitive activity, as if the child couldn't get out of a rut. Some of the rising fives were clearly bored with the available curriculum and were getting their kicks out of rough and tumble or other social activities. Some children managed a choice of activities that took them out of the teacher's orbit completely, apart from a token compliance with story sessions. Others, less boisterous, remained on the margins of activities, drifting unengaged from one space to another without ever sustaining either conversation or involvement with task or material. Though the classroom norm was happy, goal-directed use of the resources provided, enough children fell below this level, and so few rose to the heights of creativity, co-operation and challenge, that we could not feel the free play curriculum was fulfilling all our hopes.

We became interested in the children's view of the nursery classroom and their place in it, and so a sub-group of ten children (and their teachers and parents) were interviewed. We asked the children to tell us what they did at school, and what they liked doing best. We also asked them what teacher did, and whether she played with them or helped them. Teacher and child named the same activities as done by the child, particularly good agreement being shown in the case of the 'well-functioning' children. In the observations of the children at free play, all but one of the children were seen to engage in the activities they had said they did at school, six of the ten being seen to do the activity they had said they liked doing best. This suggests that the children's accounts of themselves were accurate. This is quite an interesting discovery in itself, as so many people have believed that 4 year olds can't distinguish their own view from other people's, remember events, and so forth. It has very interesting implications, too, for the children's accounts of what teachers do. If they are accurate about themselves, are they also accurate about teachers? Well, they were, in the first place, very consistent. The most commonly mentioned activities in response to the question 'What does teacher do?' were administrative – teacher 'takes the dinner money', 'puts more paint out', 'clears up'. There were fewer, but still frequent, mentions of 'reading stories'; two children mentioned educational activities – one writing, the other drawing; and a third child said that her teacher helped her with things. All these 'educational' suggestions came after the 'managing the classroom' activities that formed the main part of their accounts. Teachers for these children were kind people who provided them with nice things to play with, not people who were especially interesting to talk to or who helped them solve learning problems.

Again, this is a picture that comes out of other studies. A team from Keele observed children in nursery schools and classes, playgroups and day nurseries (personal communication from S. J. Hutt). These children spent 20–30 per cent of their time watching someone else or gazing around, not necessarily unproductively but not engaged in activity. They were more often engaged in joint activity with other children than in joint activity with adults, but more commonly still were not engaged in joint activity at all. The span of time for which they concentrated on an activity averaged under 2 minutes if no adult was involved, just over 3 minutes if an adult was there. Use of material showed a wide range of activities in the group as a whole, but many of the ways of handling materials were used by only a few children. For example, play with water included pushing boats, dropping objects in, bursting bubbles and tilting containers, but none of these occupied more than 10 seconds. The most frequent way of using water was just to pour it into an object, and even this took up considerably less time than moving objects out of the way and socialising with other children, neither of which seems an outstandingly impressive candidate for learning about the material. Fantasy play was quite rare, taking up about 15 per cent of children's time in nursery schools, and most commonly involving use of representational objects such as toy stoves and tea sets. Books were very readily accessible but were seldom used, though they were more attractive when an adult was available to read. Junk modelling and collage activities, which normally had a supervising adult present, were notable for the sustained and lively discussions which occurred – in fact the collage activity itself often seemed to be incidental to the conversation!

The London studies of Barbara Tizard and her colleagues give the same picture (Tizard *et al.*, 1976b,c; 1988). Much play in pre-school centres is at 'a rather low level', brief and simple, perhaps because children are distracted by the richness of the alternative materials available or by the many other children present, and are not under pressure from staff to persist with their activity. The staff Tizard observed rarely became involved in what children were doing, and rarely sustained a complex game or conversation. There was much less talk between children and adults than there was between child and child. Similar results come from Ruth Burberry's observations of playgroups in a suburb of Bristol (Burberry, 1980). She too found that most of children's activities were simple and of short duration, and that there was little adult–child talk, with virtually no sustained conversation. Playgroup children had more craft activities set up for them, and more structured games such as Lotto, than nursery school children did: these activities induced quite a lot of talk from adults, but most of such talk was instructions on how to make the Easter bunny or how to play the game. Finally, behaviour in the Oxfordshire groups observed by Kathy Sylva and her colleagues (Sylva *et al.*, 1980) closely resembles that seen in Stoke-on-Trent, London and Bristol – rare conversations, a lack of challenging activity, play that was disappointingly brief and simple. It seems clear that a very high proportion of children's free play over the range of pre-school centres is pleasant, keeps them busy, and does provide opportunities for learning and practising skills; but there is not much challenge, not much discovery, not much excitement, not much sustained conversation and not much persistence at working something out.

Is this because young children are too immature to be capable of better things? We would argue *not*, since they do sometimes do better in the free play setting – particularly if they are playing with adults, with an activity that has a clear structure, and with a genuine joint interest. They also seem to do better at home, though here the evidence is a bit thinner than one would like, and the clearest difference is in language, which seems to be much more restricted at school than at home in the studies of, among others, Gordon Wells and Barbara Tizard. We will also see that there are at least two ways of implementing the rich range of activities of early childhood education that make challenge more likely and sustained, excited learning more common. We describe these two strategies in Chapters 5 and 6 of this book.

Does it matter that children's play in nursery schools and other pre-school institutions tends to be repetitive, brief and unexciting, that the free play curriculum does not more often give them intellectual challenge? Are such issues important, given that the children are busy and happy? Isn't it wrong to constrain children's play even if it is done to make them think more deeply and successfully? All sorts of values come to the surface here, and the issues of educational effectiveness and of theoretical rationale that we discussed in the first chapter are relevant. We are quite clear about our values in this case: we do think intellectual excitement and rigour and creativity are good things in themselves and that self-running problem solving is an extremely desirable and useful characteristic. We think that there is strong evidence that children who have developed these characteristics so that they can use them in school are much more likely to get through the educational system successfully, and to be intellectually lively and self-confident outside it too.

We think there is strong evidence, which we look at in detail in the next chapter, that the activities of 'self-running problem solving' develop through being helped by sensitive and more skilled people, along with lots of practice, which includes feedback. What's needed is a sort of benevolent apprenticeship, with the senior partner setting things up for the junior one, helping through to a satisfactory conclusion of achievement of discovery, 'scaffolding' the learner's activities and helping to evaluate them; and letting the learner take over as he or she becomes more competent until at last the junior partner goes beyond the senior one and they can work as equals, sharing each other's knowledge as partners. As we shall see in Chapter 4, current psychological theories emphasise processes of 'metacognition' and social interaction, which were missing from the theories that underpin free play. We shall see that there is only weak evidence that the traditional free play curriculum contributes to the development of children's thinking or to their later educational achievement, though it more clearly contributes to their social skills with other children. All this convinces us that if early childhood education is to take its educational role seriously (and although *we* think it ought to be provided simply because the parents want it and the children enjoy it, there are politicians and others who will grudge the expense unless it is 'cost-effective'), the traditional free play curriculum must be re-thought.

Summary

Researchers agree that the nursery classes, nursery schools and playgroups that they have observed provide their children with a rich range of activities and materials. The children are generally found to be contented, busy, and getting along quite nicely. But three things are conspicuously rare – sustained conversation or play with an adult, high complexity of play activities, and lively purposeful involvement leading to creative exciting discovery. Children's play is often unelaborated, often brief and desultory. Some activities last longer but never amount to anything rich or fruitful. Involvement with an adult can stimulate the child's play to greater complexities and achievements, but most play does not involve adults at all, and many interactions with adults are on the level of brief and simple social routines of greeting, acknowledgement, or management of the classroom routine. Children and adults alike are busy; but there is a shortage of the intellectual endeavour and challenge that the free play curriculum is supposed to bring about.

Why is this the case? We know that young children do sometimes sustain their interest in their play for a long time, and reach high levels of excitement and discovery. The Oxfordshire observations and Barbara Tizard's data on children at home with their mothers suggest that this sort of play by children aged between 3 and 5 is particularly associated with having an adult join in the play or having a real conversation about it with the child. It is this sort of adult support that seems to be rare in the free play regime, where adult involvement in children's play is infrequent and, when it does happen, all too often fragmentary and inconclusive or too directive and didactic. If there is more responsive, scaffolding participation by adults, the children's play is more complex; if there is less, as in the playgroups that Ruth Burberry observed, the level of play activity is lower. Our study of schools and of the psychological theory and research described in the next chapter suggests to us that this is the missing ingredient in the free play curriculum. We believe that young children given more direct support from teachers (or other interested people more skilled than the child himself or herself) are more likely to find intellectual excitement in their play, to develop it fully, to acquire skills of planning, concentrating and achieving, and generally to show the characteristics of a self-running problem solver. It seems that children who do not get much of such support learn more slowly and inefficiently; that, though they sometimes have the joyful experience of learning by discovering something for themselves or working out a solution to a problem from their own agenda, they more often in a free play curriculum do not take on any particular problems and do not reflect on their activities in a way that leads to a sense of discovery. Further, so much of their play involves only themselves that they do not experience much of other people's skills, resources and challenges.

Linking what we have seen in observations to the discussion of learning theories presented in Chapter 4, the child in a free play regime has good opportunities to learn by doing, could potentially learn by reflecting on his or her own doings, but is not especially helped to do so, and has little opportunity to learn by observing adults play or having a good discussion with them. If learning by doing independent of other people was the young child's best way of learning, then the free play regime would be the most suitable sort of provision in early childhood education. In so far as children learn by reflection, by observation, by discussion and by instruction followed by reflection, the free play regime has limitations. Our discussion of how learning works suggests that these latter activities are immensely important. Thus we need to find new curricula and new teaching methods that supplement the free play curriculum and methods, and support the ways of learning that free play does not facilitate. Chapters 5 and 6 describe two possible innovations that in their different ways make up some of what is needed. We do not say they should replace free play: we do say that they certainly are invaluable extra techniques.

CHAPTER 4

How Young Children Learn

When people think about what education should be, what children should learn and when they should learn it, somewhere underpinning their thinking there are notions about *how* children learn. Many other considerations enter into decisions about education – considerations of its aims and usefulness, considerations of how much time, money and effort can be spent on it – and these may or may not be well matched with ideas about learning. Nevertheless, theories of how children learn are very much involved in questions of what 'education' should be like. It seems sensible to begin, therefore, by looking at the ideas about how children learn that are relevant to early childhood education.

Models of children's learning

One set of ideas emphasises a model of learning that is very passive. The learner is surrounded by happenings and has experiences. If two events happen together, the learner comes to associate them: for example, if every time the toddler touches the stereo his or her parents say, crossly, 'No!', he or she will learn to associate touching the stereo with parental prohibitions (and may therefore give it up). Learning colour names by being told 'that's red', 'that's blue' and so on, might be another example of passive learning. These sorts of learning depend only on things happening together, and not on any effort by the learner to interpret them, to work out what they mean. They are similar to the learning by rote which we may do at a later age when we have to study for examinations. The result of this passive learning is that we have knowledge (such as the names of colours or of the rivers of France) or habits (such as not touching other people's stereos) which are there to be used under specific circumstances and aren't thought about much. They may be strongly learned and useful, none the less.

This passive learning – just taking in a piece of information to regurgitate it later, or just reacting mechanically to an experience – is rather despised by educationists nowadays, though it was an important component of most people's formal education until very recently. (Under-fives in the late nineteenth century, like older children, learned the 3 Rs by rote, passively.) There are many reasons for this change. Among them was the evidence that suggested that even passive learners tended to work on their learning, to try to make sense of it if that was at all possible, and that if they could do this they actually dealt with the information better than the learner who just took it in like a sponge without any effort to make sense of it. Meaningless information was hard work to learn and to remember; meaningful information went in more easily and was easier to use. A neat example of this comes from studies of conditioning done with rats. Some rats were taught to associate two events: seeing a white light and receiving an electric shock to their paw. This was very hard for them to learn, even though they experienced the two events together many times. Some other rats were taught to associate a strange-tasting food with being sick: they all learned this after one experience, avoiding eating food that smelled like the nauseating one ever after. Rats are scavenging animals who need to avoid food that will make them ill: the association between food and illness was meaningful for them, while the association between light and shock was not.

There are questions to be raised about what makes a piece of information 'meaningful', which we will come back to later. The question for the moment is how information is taken in, if it is not just passively soaked up. It is not possible to give a really detailed answer to this question as a great deal more thinking and investigation have to be done, but we can point out some of the important ways in which information is handled. Piaget sketched two: assimilation and accommodation. New information is associated with what we already know in two ways: it is slightly modified so that it will fit our old knowledge better, and our old knowledge is slightly changed to take account of the new information. For example, if we have only ever seen tables with four legs, one at each corner, we may overlook the fact that a newly encountered table has one central leg, and *assimilate* it to our old idea of tables. Once we have noticed the different arrangement under the table top, however, we may *accommodate* our table concept to this new instance, and say that while most tables have four legs, at the corners, some have only one, placed centrally. With further experience of a variety of tables, the concept will be accommodated further. In the end, the most important points about a 'table' are its useful flat top and that we can sit comfortably at it; how it is supported is less crucial to the definition. If a 'table' does not have a flat top, it may be very hard to assimilate it to our concept of what tables are like. As Piaget pointed out, and as other psychologists would agree, there are limits to what we can assimilate and accommodate to, and if new information is too strange, too distant from what we already know, we will have great difficulty in learning it.

The models in practice

Current thinking about learning, then, emphasises the activity of the learner. In the practice of early childhood education, this emphasis has taken the form of an insistence on 'hands-on' experience – learning about something by direct sensory experience of it. Children are encouraged, for example, to play with water and containers of different sizes not just because they enjoy the splashing and pouring, but because they thereby experience the impossibility of getting a quart into a pint pot (or, in these post-metrication days, of getting two litres into a half-litre pot!). Hands-on experience is fine in itself, not least because it is usually enjoyable; it is clearly essential for learning many skills, particularly the physical ones – you simply cannot learn to ski except by actually practising skiing. However, it is worth doing some thinking about whether 'activity' in learning is necessarily this sort of activity. It seems fairly clear that it need not be, and that other, inner, more covert, sorts of activity may be as important in education, perhaps even more so.

In the first place, children obviously learn by observing other people's activity. In a group of pre-school children playing with plasticine, one child announces that she's going to make beads for a necklace and rolls her plasticine into little balls. Other children watch, copy, and make their own beads. Every adult who has worked with young children has seen similar incidents: children are natural observers and imitators. They are capable of learning from their observations even when they do not overtly imitate others; seeing their friends crying after being snapped at by the puppy they were teasing, they learn about the effects of annoying animals without having suffered them themselves. A person who did not learn from observation would be severely handicapped in their development; hands-on experience of everything would take far too long, and might even be dangerous.

The same arguments apply to the case of learning by being told. There are many things one cannot learn about except by being told about them – directly by another person or through books, pictures, films and so forth. Children cannot learn about dinosaurs, or about what it was like when daddy was a little boy, to name two typically interesting subjects, except by being told. At least in the case of dinosaurs, direct physical experience is unlikely to contribute much to the learning, though the learning may contribute to further physical experiences such as 'playing monsters'. Only internal experience – thinking about it – is possible and that seems to be just as possible for a 4 year old as it would be for an adult. Two American psychologists (Chi and Koeske, 1983) interviewed a little boy who was very keen on dinosaurs. His knowledge of them was greater than most adults', and organised in complex and sensible ways.

Learning is obviously possible despite little visible activity on the part of the learner. Learning from observation and learning from instruction are two important opportunities. Learning by reflecting on your own knowledge, experience and thinking is a third. Again, it is quite clear that young children do reflect on their own experience. Discussion of what has happened, and why, is common in children's conversations with familiar adults. Barbara Tizard and Martin Hughes provide some nice examples in their book *Young Children Learning* (1984). Here is one, in which Rosy (C) and her mother (M) are discussing the visit of the window-cleaner:

1C   What did Pamela say?
2M   She's having to pay everybody else's bills for the window-cleaner, 'cause they're all out.
3C   Why they all out?
4M   'Cause they're working or something.
5C   Aren't they silly!
6M   Well, you have to work to earn money, don't you?
7C   Yeah . . . If they know what day the window-cleaner come they should stay here.
8M   They should stay at home? Well, I don't know, they can't always . . .

*

1C   Mummy?
2M   Mmm.

3C Umm . . . she can't pay everybody's, er . . . all the bills to the window-cleaner, can she?

4M No, she can't pay everybody's bills . . . she sometimes pays mine if I'm out.

5C 'Cause it's fair.

6M Mm, it is.

7C Umm, but where does she leave the money?

8M She doesn't leave it anywhere, she hands it to the window-cleaner, after he's finished.

9C And then she gives it to us?

10M No, no, she doesn't have to pay us.

11C Then the window-cleaner gives it to us?

12M No, we give the window-cleaner money, he does the work for us, and we have to give him money.

13C Why?

14M Well, because he's been working for us cleaning our windows. He doesn't do it for nothing.

15C Why do you have money if you have . . . if people clean your windows?

16M Well, the window-cleaner needs money, doesn't he?

17C Why?

18M To buy clothes for his children and food for them to eat.

19C Well, sometimes window-cleaners don't have children.

20M Quite often they do.

21C And sometimes on his own to eat, and for curtains?

22M And for paying his gas bills and electricity bill. And for paying for his petrol for his car. All sorts of things you have to pay for, you see. You have to earn money somehow, and he earns it by cleaning other people's windows, and big shop windows and things.

23C And then the person who got the money gives it to people . . .

*

1M I expect the window-cleaner's going to have his lunch now.

2C He would have all *that* much lunch (stretches arms out wide) because he's been working all the time.

3M Mm . . . I expect he gets very hungry, doesn't he? I expect he goes to the pub and has some beer and sandwiches.

4C He has to pay for that.

5M   Yes, he does.

6C   Not always, though.

7M   Mm, always.

8C   Why not?

9M   They won't give him any beer and sandwiches if he doesn't have any money.

10C   But why doesn't he use his own food?

11M   Well, he might do, I don't know, perhaps he brings his own sandwiches, do you think?

12C   He go to a pub and he has his lunch some *and* he has it at his home.

13M   Oh, he wouldn't do both, no.

14C   He would do all of those a few times. But he usually go to a pub.

> Rosy's remarks in this third conversation (especially turn 6, 'Not always, though') suggest that she has only hazily grasped what she has been told, and her understanding of money transactions still seems shaky. This is not because she lacked the intellectual capacity, nor because her mother's explanations were too complex. Rather it seems likely that this conversation reveals something which is characteristic of the slow and gradual way in which a child's understanding of an abstract or complex topic is built up. It may take a considerable time, as well as several more conversations like the one above, before Rosy has grasped the complexities of the relationships involved, and she may have to return to the same topic again and again before she achieves full understanding.
>
> (Tizard and Hughes, 1984, pp.119–22)

One question that needs to be considered is what facilitates this sort of dialogue, so obviously useful for learning. Conversations like this do seem to be commoner when adult and child know each other well and are discussing a shared experience. In part, this is because the adult's knowledge of what the child's knowledge might be is more likely to be accurate. If both parties to the discussion know that Granny's cat is fat and stripy and lazy they will have more to say about it and more chance of making sense of their partner's comments, of judging their appropriateness, than if one of them does not even know whether Granny has a cat at all, let alone what its idiosyncracies are.

There may be some advantage to fostering any discussion, even if it is totally detached from reality, though little long-term advantage has been documented for such indiscriminate language interventions, but facilitating sensible discussions of a topic where both partners know something and can match utterance to reality is a much more plausible way of enhancing cognition. The two new approaches described in Chapters 5 and 6 use this principle of setting up a shared context, either by negotiation and discussion of a joint task or by using a story as a shared frame of reference and as a starting point for other activities. Task or story provide 'scaffolding' for children to build their own cognitive representation on.

We shall of course argue that 'education' involves all these sorts of learning as well as learning through activity. There might be a possible counter-argument, however, to the effect that learning by doing is the 'best' way for young children to learn. Why might this be so? What evidence do we have for it being 'best' for young children to learn through active play?

Is 'active' learning best?

Reasons why learning by doing might be 'best' for young children are linked to three main areas of ideas. First, theories about play emphasise the learning potential of spontaneous activity. Second, psychodynamic theories, like Freud's, emphasise its emotional function. Though there is in fact virtually no evidence that play has 'cathartic' or curative functions, it is certainly often enjoyable for all concerned. We value it because it is life-enhancing not because it might be therapeutic. Third, Piagetian theory centres on the developing child's thinking. Each of these areas has strongly influenced theories of early childhood education: each, when carefully examined, can be seen *not* to justify basing that education mainly on children's self-chosen activities.

Play has been heavily idealised in much of the educational writing of the last fifty years. It has been said to be spontaneous, absorbing, refreshing, enjoyable, creative and the ideal way of learning. If children aren't enabled to play as they choose, it has been claimed, their development will be impaired. Enthusiasts for play suggest that human beings have evolved so that they *need* to play in order to learn, to work off their surplus energy, to practise skills they will need in later life. While each of these claims has some truth in it, none of them is an entirely watertight reason for elevating play into *the* way of learning.

Some play is not spontaneous, absorbing, etc.; some teacher-directed activities are all these things despite being 'work' rather than 'play'. Children with very limited experience of play are sometimes impaired in their development, but so are some children whose play experience has been normal or even rich, and some children develop quite normally whatever sort of play they have had. Human beings and other animals do learn through play, use up energy, practise future skills. But they can get all these results through non-playful activities too – play is just one among many ways of learning. Is it *'better'* for learning (or for language or imagination or social adjustment) than activities that are less child-centred?

Although there has been a strong emphasis in both psychological and educational literature on the value of play for cognitive development ever since the 1920s when Susan Isaacs was perhaps the first of many to call play 'the child's work', there was little systematic attempt to examine its importance rigorously until comparatively recently. The hypothesis that play experience induces or enhances cognitive skills has now been scientifically tested in a number of areas. For example, children were asked to name uses for a material after having had 10 minutes or so of either free play with that material, or free play with a different material, or some structured training with the first material. Initially it appeared that the brief experience of playing freely with a particular material enabled children to think of more ways of using it. However, these early studies had a tester who knew what the children's experience had been, testing how many uses they could think of for the material, and it would appear that bias crept in. If the tester does not know before the test whether the child has had free play or structured experience or direct training or no play at all, there are no differences between children with different sorts of play or non-play experience. Similarly, a brief play experience with materials does not produce better use of them to solve a problem than brief training with the materials or even no experience with them at all. Again, the early results that suggested play as the best facilitator of problem solving came from studies that had not ruled out any possibility of tester bias. Regrettably, but understandably, it appears that testers who believed in the value of play, and that even 10 minutes of it would have a significant effect, may unconsciously have let this belief colour their judgement of how well the children were solving a problem or thinking up uses for an object (Smith, 1988).

Fantasy play has often been suggested as crucial to the development of cognition, language and social skills. In much-cited work, Sara

Smilansky (1968) arranged for 'play tutoring' in which nursery staff initiated and supported fantasy play with small groups of disadvantaged children, and other researchers followed her example. It generally seemed, first, that play tutoring did increase the amount of socio-dramatic play, and second, that there were good effects on all sorts of social and cognitive skills. However, again these positive results look a bit problematic. The central problem here is that the children who received 'play tutoring' designed to increase fantasy play were receiving more attention and more verbal stimulation from adults than the children in the normal classroom. It is almost certainly the case that it was the increase in attention and stimulation that produced the good effects, not that the attention and stimulation were to do with socio-dramatic play.

Thus many of the systematic attempts to show that play does have positive effects on children's cognition, language and social skills have not conclusively proved the case. It could be argued that the 'play experience' that has been evaluated was too brief or artificial to be effective, or that the wrong measures were taken. Here it may be most important to be specific about what sorts of play are expected to affect what sorts of outcome greatly and what other outcomes not at all. Tutoring in socio-dramatic play does increase social participation in such play, for example, even if its benefits for language production are much less certain. It might also be the case that some benefits are achieved after a small amount of play experience and further experience does not give the child anything useful, while other benefits come more slowly. Obviously, different materials have different potential, for example. As we discussed in Chapter 3, some children seem to exhaust the developmental usefulness of a particular material or activity but continue to choose to do it, perhaps in a highly stereotyped and repetitious way. We should be questioning ourselves about the usefulness of such activity.

The Piaget-derived justifications for learning through play seem to have three main sources. The first is Piaget's own account of play, which he saw as being a particularly clear instance of assimilation. Playing children fit their materials to their play scheme, concentrating on those characteristics that fit their theme and ignoring those that don't. A ruler can serve as a 'gun' in play, for example, because it can be pointed; the fact that it is intended for measuring things and does not go 'bang' is completely overlooked. In its earlier versions Piaget's account of 'learning' emphasised assimilation; therefore play, which is heavily assimilatory, is seen as a means of learning. Later Piagetian accounts of learning place more stress on a balance between assimilation and accommodation, which might imply that play is deficient as a way of learning in so far as it lacks the testing against reality that would make accommodation necessary.

The second concept play theorists draw from Piaget is his emphasis on the child's own activity. As we have said, the Piagetian view of learning places a heavy stress on children's activity. Being actively involved is supposed to be one of the defining characteristics of play, so again there appears to be justification here for the 'play way' of learning. But, as we have seen, other sorts of 'being active' can do very well for learning, and the most recent version of Piagetian theory emphasises 'doing' less and 'thinking about what has been done' more. Being actively engaged in doing something, experiencing it, is not sufficient for learning much from it.

The third Piagetian concept which justifies play is what one might call 'readiness'. Piaget saw learning as controlled and limited by development: unless children had developed to a point where they were ready, they would not be able to do the thinking, assimilation and accommodation that are necessary for learning. There was no point in trying to accelerate their learning by trying to teach them skills or information they were not ready for – indeed, to try to teach might harm the child's own development. Because in play-centred education teaching children is de-emphasised, harming their development by accelerating them is unlikely. Since children are free to choose their own activity, and it is assumed they will choose to do only things they are 'ready ' to do (or at least if they choose things they are not 'ready' for they will soon give them up), free play looks like maximising the amount of activity that children are 'ready' to learn from.

This concept is perhaps the strongest of the 'Piagetian' reasons for encouraging play as the medium for early childhood education. However, it too is not completely sound. In the first place, it is impossible to define whether children are 'ready' to learn something or not before we have given them a fair opportunity to learn it. Obviously we can be pretty certain that a 6 month old is not 'ready' to learn to play the trombone; but how do we know whether a 4 year old is 'ready' to learn to read? In some cases we can identify early stages or useful prerequisites for the skill we are interested in, and we may know that the child does not yet show an ability to do these things. But the 'readiness' question has just been pushed back a bit in the sequence of how the skill is acquired. This child is not 'ready' to read, as we know that he or she does not yet manage to recognise any words at all, and we have good grounds for believing that doing this comes before reading; but do we know whether or not the child is 'ready' to be helped to recognise some words? Unless we provide an opportunity to learn to recognise words – the child's name, for example, or words labelling familiar objects – we do not know whether the child is 'ready' to learn. If we assume that he or she is 'not ready', and do not offer the opportunity, the child probably will not learn. But we cannot be sure that this confirms the 'not readiness'; it might be that the child has not learned purely because there was no opportunity to learn. Almost always, if a teacher decides that a child is 'ready' to learn something and gives the child a fair opportunity, the child learns successfully. The problem is not one simply of whether the child is 'ready' or not, but of how the opportunity to learn is presented and managed by the teacher.

Social sources of children's learning

Here it is useful to introduce a concept from the work of the Russian psychologist, Vygotsky (1978). He disagreed with Piaget's view that thinking and knowing were very largely the result of an individual reflecting on his or her own activity, with other people's influence being of minor importance. Vygotsky emphasised how much we learn from interacting with other people, how much we are helped by what we are taught and by what we see other people do. For Vygotsky, knowledge is social, and what we are able to do is much more a matter of our upbringing and education than of our inborn potential: development is very much a product of the child's participation in the social world.

Piaget himself regarded social interaction and transmission as one of the major factors behind cognitive development, but he placed much less emphasis on it than on the child's own self-generated activities. He saw thought as 'egocentric', developing within each individual rather than as a product of interaction between individuals. Once language is acquired, the social environment can influence a child's cognition, but it 'enriches' the patterns of thought that the child has already constructed. The origins of cognitive development are in the child not in the social world.

More recently, many of the researchers involved in the criticism and development of Piagetian theory have concerned themselves with the role of social interaction in cognitive development. Some have examined the contribution of seeing your own belief conflict with a peer's belief, which Piaget himself proposed as a source of cognitive conflict that might fuel further development. Some have examined the social meaning of the test situations that Piaget used, and have concluded that if the situations were modified so that they were not socially anomalous but made what Margaret Donaldson (1978) called 'human sense', children would show much better cognitive performance.

Both these developments of Piagetian theory have implications for teachers working with young children. Discussion of ideas, and co-operation in problem solving, may facilitate thinking, and very careful consideration of test questions and test settings may help us to avoid underestimating children. But beyond these points, which are still comparatively Piagetian, there is the possibility of a more radical re-appraisal of how social interaction and transmission affect cognition. Perhaps the social context might play a very active role indeed in determining cognitive development: the cognitive skills of child and adult develop and are used within their experience and knowledge of everyday social events. This is the core of Vygotsky's position.

Vygotsky's work was done immediately after the Russian Revolution and was curtailed when he died, comparatively young, of tuberculosis. Other Russian psychologists have carried on on similar lines, but only a very small proportion of all this work has reached a Western audience, and only comparatively recently. Vygotsky believed that human mental development was in the direction from outside in, from external social and meaningful behaviour between people to the complex internal forms of mental life. Language, in particular its use to communicate meanings during social interaction, provided an initial structure for children's cognitive activity. Later on such language becomes internalised as the child's thinking becomes more independent of adult support. Thus what is initially communicative speech turns inwards to become the basis of inner speech, though obviously children continue to use language externally to communicate their thought to others as well as using language internally to help themselves with their own thought. This is virtually the opposite of Piaget's position, and Vygotsky is placing much more emphasis on the support that the social context gives to an individual's cognition. This account suggests that early discussion and early reflection on cognition may be facilitated by adult–child dialogue and joint action, which Piaget would have thought much less appropriate than adults providing minimal constraint on children's free play.

This emphasis leads to a strong interest in education and a much more positive view of it than Piaget had. So far as the 'readiness' issue is concerned, Vygotsky makes the important suggestion that we should think of the child being at *two* levels of development. One is familiar, the 'actual' or 'present' level of development – that is, what the child can do on its own, without the support or instruction of adults. The other, much less Piagetian, is the 'potential' level of development – that is, what the child can achieve in collaboration with adults or other more skilled people given the optimum help, guidance, encouragement, etc. Normally this will be more advanced than the 'present' level: the gap between the two levels indicates what the child is ready to learn, given adult help. Vygotsky calls this area the 'zone of next development' or 'zone of proximal development'. Teaching that is directed towards getting children to do *without* help what they can at present do only *with* help is the best way to improve development. Vygotsky's approach implies that it is right for the teacher to intervene in the child's learning much more than Piaget would approve of. One reason for intervening is to discover what the child's 'zone of next development' is; another is to bring the present level of development up into this zone. Most importantly, if children's development involves a lot of learning from other people, teachers should be teaching *and* they should be seen to be doing things that are at the child's 'potential' level. A curriculum that centres on free play may not allow these sorts of activities, and if it is insisted that children cannot benefit from other people's experience, they will have to spend ages discovering the wheel (or whatever) all over again. Adult prompting, pointing out and modelling should reduce wasted effort and extend children's understanding beyond what they can do for themselves.

Bruner has developed the relevant metaphor of 'scaffolding' (Bruner, 1983; Wood, 1988). A more expert person, adult or older peer, helps the less expert person through learning how to deal with a problem, initially providing a great deal of support, which is gradually reduced as the learner becomes able to take on the task more independently. This sort of interaction, where the child moves from being a spectator to being a participant on increasingly equal terms, and eventually perhaps to initiating and directing the activity, seems to be what happens in the acquisition of language, which, as we have seen, is for Vygotsky a near relation and a crucial influence on cognition and learning. Bruner believes that one important aspect of the development of language and cognition is the use they make of familiar structured social interactions such as peekaboo games and looking at books. The child also learns about shared attention to a common goal so that joint activities can be co-ordinated, intentions communicated and plans discussed. Frameworks that establish the general nature of the topic and the interaction reduce uncertainty and provide possible things to do when the next step is not quite certain. They also provide helpful cues for recalling what has been done and so for learning what was successful and what had less satisfactory consequences.

Here we will mention another new general theory of how early cognitive development proceeds. Katherine Nelson has looked at children learning about the routine aspects and regular happenings of the social world (Nelson, 1986). She describes 'generalised event representations' or 'scripts' which children use to organise both their ideas about how their world works and their participation in it. Such 'scripts' are developed quite remarkably quickly. In one study, 5 year olds were asked 'what do you do in school?' on their *second* day there. Their answers were generalised, abstract and correct as to the order of events. Here is one example from a study by Robin Fivush:

> 'Play. Say hello to the teacher and you do reading or something. You can do anything you want to. Clean up, then you play some more and then clean up. And then you go to the gym or playground. And then you go home. You have your lunch and then you go home. And you go out the school, and you ride on the bus or the train and go home.'
>
> (Fivush, 1984, p.1708)

Scripts support and structure cognition rather as adult 'scaffolding' does. They provide a sequence of events that can be used for remembering, comparing and predicting what happens. Different items can be slotted in at the appropriate point and this may be a basic part of early categorisation – going home by bus or train, for example, is at the root of the 'means of transport' category in Robin Fivush's child. Scripts give a child a set of expectations that structure and support talking about or enacting the event they refer to, and they free attention to concentrate on unfamiliar aspects of the event, or its importance at this particular moment. They are often social scripts, so other 'actors' will contribute to the sequence of events and to how the child makes sense of the script. Good stories use these sorts of expectations, and children quickly learn the general 'script' so that they can predict what comes next and interpret the motives and feelings of the characters. Similarly, taking part in familiar routines with adults, discussing joint activity and both planning and reviewing what is done will facilitate children's understanding and competence. They may be able to employ basic cognitive skills much better when the situation has a 'script' that makes sense to them than when the demand lacks context and is too abstract to be understood.

'Metacognition' and young children's learning

There has been another shift of emphasis in ideas about learning which we will mention here. In current developmental psychology and educational theory there is a lot of interest in children's ideas about their own thought processes, their own ability to remember, and various similar topics, which have collectively been called 'metacognition'.

Metacognition involves a range of different psychological contents. It includes being aware of your own cognition, knowing whether you understand or not, have remembered something or forgotten it, at this particular moment. It also includes knowing about your own skills and being able to see how well they match up to the demands of a task. Finally, and perhaps most importantly, it includes regulating cognition, for example planning how to do a task, monitoring progress on it, asking for further information when you feel you need it, checking the solution. These sorts of skills and knowledge have recently been seen as one of the most important areas of cognitive development, in part because there seems to be a dramatic development from little metacognition in early childhood to quite extensive and sophisticated metacognition in adolescence and adulthood.

Children as young as 2 may show some rudimentary metacognitive awareness, particularly awareness that there is a discrepancy between what they intended to happen and what has actually happened. At this age they will often become distressed if they are asked to imitate too complex an action: where a younger child will happily imitate only part of the action, a 2 year old may dissolve into floods of tears at being asked to combine two imitative actions that she or he can do separately but not together. Metacognitive knowledge such as this is no doubt one source of the requests for help (or alternatively to be allowed to 'do it my own self') and of the statements of 'I can't do it' which arise in children's play. Young children develop simple plans and strategies for solving problems, commonly repetitive trial and error rather than a more planned investigation. Another common and sensible strategy is to seek help from a more skilled person – parent, teacher or peer.

Children are very commonly novices on tasks where adults have become experts with many well-learned routines. It is part of the process of education to facilitate the child's sharing of this expertise. It is important to recognise that it is both *specific* expertise – how to paint a straight line on the paper – and generalised expertise – how to hold tools, adjust their use to the particular task, judge where to start and where to stop, and so forth. A general 'feel' for the task as a whole is crucial. The component parts of the task may overload the capabilities of novices so that they do not have time or space for higher metacognitive activity and may not be aware that it would be useful. Here an adult or expert can be invaluable both through providing the 'scaffolding' we discussed earlier, and as someone who can tactfully point out that using a metacognitive strategy, such as deliberately trying to memorise the important information, has in fact improved performance. Children can learn to use metacognitive tactics but they normally only bother to do so if they have convincing evidence that it is worth the effort. Seeing older people make explicit efforts to remember, plan, review their learning and so forth probably enhances metacognitive development, particularly when these efforts are seen to pay off. One important aspect of cognitive development is a progress from cognition supported by, and regulated by, other people more skilled than oneself, to cognition that is relatively independent and self-regulated. A great deal of thinking and learning may remain a social activity, but the social participation changes from being like a novice learning from an expert to being more of a co-operation between near equals.

While most of the research has been done with children of junior school age or older, the idea that the deliberate thinking through of problems is important surely applies to younger children too. Thinking about your thinking seems to be an effective way of getting better at it, and also to be a source of self-confidence.

CHAPTER 5

The Dialogue Approach: Tutorial Teaching

Aims and philosophy

The main reason why children come to school is to learn and the main reason why teachers are there is to help them to do so. Of course, this help should often be indirect, as when the teacher provides appropriate materials, an encouraging environment, or a helpful suggestion. But there are times when children need direct teaching too. Many children, perhaps through experience at home, take to this very readily. Others do not seem to realise for themselves how they could be using the classroom environment or, indeed, how the teacher could help them. Such children, moreover, seem to get little benefit from brief and incidental contacts with their teacher. They need help in seeing what the teacher wants of them and how s/he can be of use. Some children find the teacher a strange person who speaks differently from themselves and it takes time and careful work to help them set up fruitful relationships with the teacher. Many of them, too, though they are not lacking in most language skills or in curiosity, do not naturally fall into the *exploratory* and *expressive* modes that will be so helpful to them in their later education and that will help them develop towards Donaldson's 'disembedded thinking' (Donaldson, 1978; and see Chapter 4 this volume). In other words, these children are not used to working things out, or to explaining them. The dialogue approach has been specially designed for such children; but we think it helpful, and recommend its use, with all children. Even the best-functioning child reaches a point quite often of needing encouragement to go further, to think things out, or to explain them to him/herself or to an adult. It is just this thinking things out and putting them into words that is the essence of the teaching approach.

However, we go further than this. What we are trying to do is to help children to become 'self-running' in their intellectual development. We want them to stand on their own feet, to ask their own questions about the properties of objects, about their suitability for different purposes, about how to make things and about how to control their immediate surroundings. We want them to listen to language and to use it themselves, so as to 'fix' their skills; in other words, so as to know what choices they have made and why, and to remember them. Finally, we want them to regard themselves as competent investigators whose business it is to understand the world. In this sense, the dialogue approach is most closely allied to 'science' as a curriculum area, even at pre-school level.

Clearly, language is important in the approach, but ours is not a 'language programme'. Language is an enormously useful tool. There is, however, no point in improving children's language for its own sake. We are in the business of improving language only because this helps children so much to achieve their purposes. Of course, we do have long-term goals for children in our minds. But teaching that is aimed at long-term goals and not also rooted very firmly in present needs soon becomes sterile. Not only that, the children will not see its purpose and will, quite rightly, lose interest. So the tasks in which we seek to involve children have to be tasks that they see to be meaningful. Similarly, when we want children to explain, this has to be because the explanation will be of benefit to them – and they will have to be able to see how this is so.

There are many occasions when the teacher can help children to think productively in the total class situation. At other times, the teacher can work with them in small groups. Our teaching approach is designed specifically for work in the one-to-one situation, where the teacher is engaged with a single child. It is based very closely on the method developed by Marion Blank (Blank, 1973) for regular use in individual work with poorly functioning children. Her teachers would see the child alone, away from the classroom, for sessions of about 15 minutes. In the Open University project (Meadows and Cashdan, 1983) we employed this method in initial working with the teacher. However, in our view it is not necessary, or even desirable, to take the child away from the normal classroom context for this kind of work. Once teachers are experienced and confident with the technique, we see them as using it in the classroom, still with individual children, but for varying periods. Usually, work with one child may go on for only 2 or 3 minutes, or at the most for 7 or 8. The work may be specifically planned by the teacher, or it may arise out of the child's own freely chosen activity, but it is a major principle of our approach that this interaction should take place in children's normal setting as a recognised part of their routine. In other words, each one of the children comes to expect the teacher to spend short periods specifically with him/her, exploring a problem that is for that period theirs and theirs alone.

Of course, there is a big difference between using the teaching method artificially, outside the classroom, and making it a flexible part of the daily routine. Certainly, this transition was a point of particular concern to all the teachers in our project. Furthermore, the obvious question is 'How can I find the time to work with one child in a classroom with more than twenty others all asking for my attention at once?' Our answer is that this needs careful management, but that it can be done – as most of the teachers in our first research group came to agree. In the longer term, dialogue work becomes so much a part of the teacher's regular working pattern that it is no longer thought of as a separate activity: teaching is 'naturally' and flexibly divided between individual, small group and whole class working.

We shall now introduce the teaching approach by discussing the main principles around which it is built. In the following section these principles will be put into the context of a typical teaching sequence. Then we will list and illustrate two of the main types of activity the teacher needs to be aware of: the use of *demands* and of *follow-ups*. After summarising the purpose of the approach and what we hope it achieves we give a detailed example, with illustrative comments.

Principles in working with the child

We use eight major principles:

1. Teaching to an appropriate range of cognitive demands

Whenever we ask a child a question we are making a 'demand' on that child. This can be at quite a low level (e.g. 'What's this?' 'What colour is it?') or at a very difficult level (e.g. 'What made you say the little girl was pleased?'). If the teacher's questions are always at a level that is rather simple for the child to cope with, then the child will not be extended. Conversely, if questions are always pitched at too high a level, there will be the frustration of continual failure. The teacher who is aware of the range of possible levels of demand is in a good position to vary questions appropriately, striking the best balance between extending the child and consolidating their existing knowledge. Such a teacher is also able to work diagnostically; that is, to vary the demands made in a specific way to suit the needs of a particular child. One child may function quite well, except when too much stress is placed on memory. Another may comprehend language well but be poorer at expression. So the teacher needs to know what are appropriate demands for each child within the range of possible types of questions.

2. Managing the response

Varying the demand is a beginning, but what to do when the demand is not met? In other words, the problem with the 'poorly functioning' child is often the failure to manage an appropriate answer to the question. The teacher's prime need is for an array of techniques for following up inadequate answers. S/he needs to have ready a series of possible *simplifications* or other means of putting the question again, or reorganising it so that the child is now able to answer. There is nothing worse for both teacher and child than abandoning an approach because the child has not managed an appropriate answer and the teacher is uncertain what to do next:

T   What a lovely dress. Is it new? Did your mother make it? Aren't you pleased with it?
C   Yes.
T   Or did she buy it from Marks and Spencers?
C   Mummy . . . (tails off).
T   I do like the flowers on it. What are they?
C   Flowers.
T   What would you like to do now?

The child's first reply ('yes') is insufficient. We don't know (nor did the child probably) which of the teacher's questions she was answering. The second is inadequate and not followed up (she *may* have meant that her mother had made the dress). The third time she probably mis-understood the teacher, but again the reply is not built upon. Obviously, it only takes three or four such exchanges for the teacher to terminate the conversation, by patting the child on the head (literally or figuratively) and passing on to someone else. The child is left with a feeling of bewilderment, if not outright failure.

As with the range of demands, the types of follow-up or simplification, once listed (see below), are obvious. But it is very important for the teacher to have an appropriate one ready. In learning how to do this, the teacher is learning how to match teaching to the precise point at which the child is currently functioning. Indeed, this is the central skill of teaching. So much so, that we will now pause to consider this issue further.

Why match levels?

One of the most important things in teaching is the need to tailor one's approach quite precisely to the child. This is a particularly central task in working with nursery school age children, and also one of the most difficult.

It is important to match the child's level for several reasons, which relate closely to the main aims of the nursery school experience. The broadest aim is to encourage the child to enjoy learning, finding out and understanding. The best (easiest and longest-lasting) learning takes place when there is a small difference between what each child can do already and what they are asked to do or learn (see Hunt, 1969). Vygotsky (1978) called this the 'zone of proximal development'. If the discrepancy is very small – if the task is one that is already well mastered – then there is no challenge in the situation, no need to make any effort and no new learning will take place. At best the child will have an opportunity to practise a skill already possessed; at worst there will be the boredom of being asked to do something that is too easy. If, at the other extreme, the discrepancy is too great, if the task is far beyond the child's repertoire of skills, then the challenge of the situation is overwhelming and frightening; the child knows that success is impossible and does not even try. At best, the one opportunity for learning is lost; more likely, the child will either see themselves as a failure or see the teacher as an insensitive person, perhaps from a remote world, making impossible and meaningless demands.

If the first reason for matching the child's level concerns this basic psychological mechanism of the best size of discrepancy for learning and motivation, the second is the related matter of what education involves. An important feature of nursery school teaching is that the teacher is providing the children with their first experience of school, which is going to occupy a good part of their waking hours for at least the next eleven years and which may well determine the course of their entire adult life. It could be an overstatement to say that their experience of nursery school will determine what they make of their later schools, but certainly, as we saw earlier, the nursery school can 'set them up' with expectations of school and teacher that will strongly influence their later reactions to education.

The nursery school can also have a very important influence on the child's self-picture. It is disturbing that a child of 3 can have learned to think of him/herself as a failure, as someone who can't succeed so doesn't try, but this certainly does happen, and children's experience of adults' demands is an important part of the development of their self-image.

So matching the child's level and asking them to do things that are just slightly difficult is important for several different reasons:

(1) *the match–mismatch theory of motivation and learning*: the belief that a small intellectual effort of extension is the best situation for learning and perfecting the child's understanding of their world.

(2) *children's idea of school*: it is desirable that they should see it as an interesting place with adults who make demands that can be met successfully, who are sensitive to the child's capacities and interested in them as individuals.

(3) *the child's self-image*: it is desirable that children should meet a high proportion of success experiences in school so that they continue to see themselves as capable of understanding and finding out, and their curiosity and liveliness of mind are not discouraged.

3. Developing a sequential theme

A successful interchange needs to go on for long enough to engage both child and teacher. It has to have possibilities for development and for flexibility. So questions on colours or shapes are not always the most fruitful ones. Nor are requests for simple description or labels often referred to as 'display' questions – 'What's that?' 'What sort is it?' Usually it's better to engage the child in a meaningful task – tying up a parcel, making a drink, even drawing a picture together.

4. Selecting appropriate materials

It follows from this that the likeliest subjects are to be found among real-life needs. What are meaningful and worthwhile activities for a 3 or 4 year old? Usually, tasks associated with daily life – food, outings, washing, sleeping, and so on. So it makes most sense to centre a session around washing a doll, cutting up an apple, icing a biscuit. Again, abstract sorting tasks are less likely to appeal and they offer relatively little opportunity for finding out about the world around us, discussing it and arriving at conclusions.

5. Checking the child's response

If conversations between teacher and child are to be real opportunities for sharing, then it is best to stay within the limits of what is present and can be checked up upon, or at least to restrict the conversation to shared memories. The problem is that it is perfectly possible to have a fluent conversation about something not present – say, grandmother's black cat. This may provide ample opportunity for language practice. But if the teacher does not know whether grandmother *has* a cat, how it behaves, or what it is like (or, as in the example above, who made the dress or where it came from), then there can be no certain meeting of minds on the subject. If the child says the apple is harder than the ball, teacher and child can experiment with these together. If s/he says that grandmother's cat is bigger than uncle's dog, there is no way of verifying this claim. Of course fantasy is valuable. What we are arguing is that there is a place for controlled experiment and exploration too. And there is nothing that concentrates the mind better than a shared topic, present in the here and now, which can be worked on and through together.

6. Keeping the child active

Young children learn by doing; they need to be active as well as to observe. So we emphasise creating things, reaching an end product, indulging in physical action. Young children do not sustain abstract conversation well. They thrive on having something to do physically – and as long as the physical activity does not swamp everything else, this is the best way to work.

7. Pacing the session

If the child responds correctly to every question asked of him/her, the session is likely to be almost as much a failure as if they get everything wrong. This seems paradoxical at first, but in fact it is good sense. For learning to occur, there must be an awareness of something not known. So the teacher should be challenging children with questions they cannot answer – and then helping them to find the answers. Probably, in an ideal session, the child should be faced with questions that are really taxing for up to a third of the time. These need to be spread carefully, hence the word *pacing*. Normally a session should begin at a high level of demand, with a good proportion of difficult questions, but should become rather easier towards the end when the consolidating and rounding-off point is being reached. The child then goes away with a feeling of success and achievement.

8. *Giving the session a shape*

An interchange is most likely to develop positively if it begins with a clear statement of intent, agreed upon by both teacher and child. This may well be suggested by the teacher; after all, the teacher is the mature partner in the discussion. The agreement needs to be at two levels: that of action and that of cognitive purpose – 'Shall we cut an apple up *and* find out how everyone can have a piece?', 'Shall we take it apart *and* find out how it works?'.

Then comes the main development in which the theme of the session is developed and worked through. At the end, there is a brief drawing together of the threads. This demands an apparently casual, but very important, revision. 'Let's just see what we found out? What did we do first . . . ?' The teacher and the child run through the session, reminding each other of the salient events and discoveries. The session ends positively, with a feeling of achievement on both sides.

Planning

In the early stages of dialogue work, teachers choose to 'target' a particular child and plan a session in general terms with appropriate materials and concepts in mind. These always have to be used flexibly in response to the reactions and pace of the child but they form an agenda and a platform from which to move off. Many teachers find activities that would occur naturally in many homes good to work with – icing a biscuit, washing dolls' clothes. Those create natural situations for exploration which start from the child's experience but can move forward from it – to anything, say, from how to get the doll's face clean to the properties of washing powders. With experience, such props and preparation become less necessary. The teacher becomes more of an automatic diagnostician – picking out a good point at which to join a child's own activity ('Shall I come and do it with you?' 'What can we find out?' – and note the double agenda that we always favour: explicit practical tasks and explicit intellectual purposes). With practice, too, she can take up on the point that a dialogue with that child reached yesterday or last week, following up creative ideas, vocabulary, fostering interests, etc. It may sound critical to say so, but in the 'mainstream' classroom teachers just do not often do this (see Chapter 3 for some of the evidence). When they do work in this way, the rewards in helping and understanding individual children are enormous.

Goals

Although it may often seem obvious whether or not learning has occurred in a dialogue session, it clearly helps if the teacher has some general idea of the child's developmental level, which s/he can progressively refine as teaching progresses from day to day and month to month. It helps greatly if such ideas can be tied to a firm idea of the cognitive curriculum – what 3 and 4 year olds should be doing – and to a clear picture of where they should be heading – that is, a model of the well-functioning 5 year old (and onwards).

The first of these has been explored by researchers such as David Weikart and his team (Weikart *et al.*, 1978; see Hohmann *et al.*, 1979). Indeed, in general terms the Weikart nursery prescription of plan–do–review much resembles the outline of our approach to dialogue. Weikart and co. offer a list of some fifty 'key experiences' that should be offered in their 'cognitive curriculum'. These range from 'exploring activity with all the senses', to 'relating pictures . . . to read things', to 'having fun with language: rhyming, making up stories', etc. Such lists of experiences are worth considering to ensure a full and balanced curriculum, much of which can be experienced through the dialogue approach.

The other question – where the child should be heading – can be monitored by the use of checklists such as the developmental sequences which started with Gesell and have been taken further in such publications as the National Children's Bureau's Development Guides. Although not as detailed, Marion Blank's 'scale of abstraction' helps to organise one's thinking about children's development (Blank *et al.*, 1978). The scale has two aspects, with four levels of abstraction, demonstrating how, as abstraction increases, language moves steadily away from a tight relationship to perception, becoming increasingly 'disembedded' to use Margaret Donaldson's term. The scales may be most easily understood by reference to Figures 5.1 and 5.2. Blank and her colleagues explain the stages as follows.

> The demands cover a range of ideas. What we will do here is organize the demands according to the levels of abstraction that they represent. The first level of abstraction is *Matching Perception*. Some of the teacher's verbalizations that fit into this level are:
>
> > What is this?
> > What things do you see on the table?
> > I'd like to have one.
> > Please give me the potholder.
>
> At the second level of abstraction, *Selective Analysis of Perception*, some of the key demands are:
>
> > Now we'll need a bowl to mix all these things together.
> > What shape is the bowl?
> > Oh, look how they are spreading out!
> > Let's think of some other things that we can bake in the oven.
>
> In the next level of abstraction, *Reordering Perception*, the demands on the child are:
>
> > Tell me what we put in the bowl before we added the egg.
> > Show me the part of the egg that we don't eat.
>
> At the fourth level of abstraction, *Reasoning about Perception*, the child is asked to theorize, explain, and rationalize. Continuing the illustration of the cookies, formulations at this level are:
>
> > Why don't we eat that part?
> > What will happen to the cookies when we put them in the oven?
> > We'll need to use a potholder because otherwise we'll burn our hands.
>
> (Blank *et al.*, 1978, pp. 17–18)

We are not suggesting that teachers should try to get their pupils through the NCB's sequence, or push them determinedly from matching perception through to reasoning about it. But we do know that such lists and scales provide a useful backcloth of general expectations against which to develop one's day-to-day work with children.

Figure 5.1   *The perceptual–language distances underlying the scale of abstraction*

	LEVEL				
	I	II	III	IV	
perceptual					perceptual
language distance	Matching Perception	Selective Analysis of Perception	Reordering Perception	Reasoning about Perception	
					language distance

Perceptual represents the material available to the child; language represents the verbal formulations of the teacher.

Source: Blank *et al.,* (1978), p.17.

Figure 5.2   *An overview of the scale of abstraction for pre-school discourse*

I	Matching Perception	reporting and responding to salient information	What things do you see on table?
II	Selective Analysis of Perception	reporting and responding to delineated and less salient cues	What shape is the bowl?
III	Reordering Perception	using language to restructure perceptual input and inhibit predisposing responses	Show me the part of the egg that we don't eat.
IV	Reasoning about Perception	using language to predict, reflect on, and integrate ideas and relationships	What will happen to the cookies when we put them in the oven?

Source: Blank *et al.,* (1978), p. 18.

The teaching sequence

It should be stressed again that we are not suggesting that teachers spend all their time in the nursery classroom giving individual children 'special' sessions and giving up all their other normal activities. Far from it; all we are recommending is that teachers add this possibility to their normal range of activities, fitting in these sessions with children they feel would benefit either opportunistically when a particular child is engaged in an activity that seems to lend itself, or by planning appropriately for one or more of the children in advance. What we are suggesting is that a teaching sequence will be far more successful, providing both child and teacher with purpose and achievement, if it has a well-defined shape. This will normally have four main features:

1. Deciding on an appropriate task

This should be agreed mutually, whether the teacher has planned the activity in advance or whether it is a suggested extension of something the child has already chosen to do. The important thing is that the teacher seizes the potential of the particular activity for this child, at this moment.

2. Introducing the task

Teacher and child then decide together (with the teacher normally taking the lead) what they are going to do and what may be achieved from it. So there is a clear agenda: we are going to ice a biscuit and find out how to do it properly, or we are going to paint the table and find out about paint and tables and about how to make a good job of it. Note that there are two parts – the activity *and* the learning involved in it. Both are important and both are part of the shared agenda.

3. Preserving the sequence

The teacher uses an appropriate range of demands, adjusts simplifications or other follow-ups according to the responses given, and paces the session gently but with a sure touch. S/he does not hesitate to discourage the child from giving up or going off at a tangent. This does not mean bullying or keeping children at a task when it is no longer working. It does mean not being frightened of suggesting going on for a little longer or keeping to the task in hand even when the child has thought of something else. Obviously, the teacher will use their professional judgement and allow a change of activity or distraction if it seems that the child needs this, or that the session had better come to an end. But we have found that, with experience, teacher and child enjoy staying at an activity rather than going off before it has been worked through.

4. Reviewing what has been done

When the activity terminates naturally, or when the teacher judges that enough has been achieved, the activity and associated learning are reviewed. This gives children a chance to consolidate new ideas and vocabulary and to organise their memory. It also establishes for them that what has been done has a value and meaning to the teacher as well as to themselves. Sometimes an immediate review is not possible, perhaps for practical reasons, perhaps through loss of interest. It may nevertheless be really valuable to have one later on in the morning or even on the next day. Children often remember a surprising amount and positively enjoy going through the sequence with the teacher.

Demands

Let us now look at a sample of the most typical cognitive demands made upon pupils. The list is not exhaustive, but it does cover the main areas. Remember that it is not being suggested that the teacher should use all these types of question. Rather, the teacher should be aware of which ones are typically being used and be ready to adjust up and down the list, as well as to maintain a reasonable variety. The demands are arranged very roughly in ascending order from simple to complex. Here are titles and examples for some simpler ones:

(1) *Labelling and simple function*: 'What is it?' 'What do you do with it?'
(2) *Memory*: 'What did you just see?' 'What was that over there?'
(3) *Description*: 'What is happening in the picture?'
(4) *Non-verbal demand*: 'Feel that.' 'What is it?'
(5) *Imitation*: 'Like that' (demonstrates). 'Now do what I did.' (Note that this is still a cognitive demand although the child is not asked to say anything.)
(6) *Incidental memory*: 'What else was there on the tray?' 'What else did you notice?'
(7) *Delay*: 'Before you drink the milk, show me the cup.'
(8) *Visual search*: 'Look at this tray (or picture). Find me a rabbit; find two screws.'

Now for some rather harder demands:

(9) *Comparative analysis*: 'How is this one different from the one we just looked at?' 'What is the difference between these two (a toy bus and a toy van)?'

(10) *Cause and effect*: 'What made the room cold?'

(11) *Imagery/prediction*: 'Where would the doll be if it fell off the table?' 'What will happen if I turn the bottle over?'

(12) *Means–ends relationships*: 'What can I use to reach the top shelf?'

(13) *Higher level/logical relationships*: 'If I take two, how many will be left?' 'If you gave me another four, how many would there be?'

(14) *Rationale*: 'How did you know the little girl was upset?'

(15) *Word skills*: 'What rhymes with train?'

Incidentally, these headings remind us what complicated thinking some 3 and 4 year olds are capable of. In the abstract, it seems unlikely that such young children could explain causal relationships or provide a rationale. But, given the right context, even a 3 year old may be able to explain how s/he knew someone was feeling sick (see no. 14 above). As we said earlier, the list is not exhaustive; you should be able to add other types of demands yourself. You may also find that some of those given appear to overlap – in some contexts they do. Significantly also, you will find that particular demands vary in difficulty according to the situation and to how they are worded.

Follow-ups

Follow-up techniques are entirely obvious once they are pointed out. The merit of this list is that it reminds us of the many possible ways of helping the child who does not manage a response to the original demand. They should be used quite freely. It is most helpful for teachers to tape-record an occasional session with a child and then note the follow-ups they have been using, whether they managed to help the child to respond without simply feeding in the answer and what they *might* have done in some of the 'sticky' passages!

(1) *Attention-getting, or recapturing*: This technique may be divided into three sub-categories:

    (a) focus – the teacher touches the child, makes eye contact, says 'What did I say?'

    (b) s/he may use delay – 'wait until I finish.'

    (c) s/he may repeat the demand, either using identical words, or adding stress – 'Put the *glass* on the *table*.'

(2) *Rephrasing*: Here significant words are changed: 'Pick up the box' instead of 'Lift the box'.

(3) *Giving part of the answer*: 'What's a bucket for?' No response. 'A bucket can carry . . . ?' No response. 'A bucket can carry w . . . ?' Note an important principle here – the teacher does not supply the whole of the answer, but moves progressively nearer to it, always hoping that the pupil will eventually answer him/herself. The 'feed' is avoided; that is, saying 'It's to carry water, isn't it?' – this is merely an invitation to say 'yes'.

(4) *Subdividing the task*: The teacher builds a tower of blocks, a green, a yellow, a red. The pupil is at a loss as to how to copy it. 'Right,' says the teacher, 'show me the *bottom* one.'

(5) *Helping to discard a wrong or meaningless answer*: This can be done by demonstration or by supplying a verbal cue. The biscuit is too big to go in the cup. 'Why won't it go in the cup?' The child says 'Because it's too hard'. The teacher breaks it in half – 'Why will it go in now?'

(6) *Presenting comparisons*: The teacher may provide a strong contrast, making the comparison very easy: 'Did we open the door, the wall, the ceiling?' or a weak contrast: 'Did it go under the *table*?' Or a model: 'Is it like this one?'

(7) *Giving information or a demonstration*: 'That's one – now show me.' Or, 'Like this. Now you do it.'

(8) *Asking for a fuller response*: 'What did we do then?' 'Bucket.' 'Yes, what did we do with the bucket?' Or the child points vaguely. Teacher says, 'Show me exactly where.'

(9) *Repeating a demonstration*: This is an extension of no. 1 above. It may help the child to think things through if s/he has become confused.

(10) *Relating the unknown to the known*: The child cannot explain what will happen to the apples in the pan – so the teacher asks 'What happened to the *potatoes* when we cooked them?' One has to be careful here not to make the second question *harder*. If the child is puzzled by a question about a spoon, it may help to ask, 'Well what does a *fork* do then?'

(11) *Directing action to learn significant characteristics*: 'Turn it over then' – the child has to follow directions, not just nod at an explanation.

(12) *Focusing on relevant features*: 'Why did you take your hand away from the stove?' No response. 'What did it *feel* like?'

(13) *Substituting action for verbal response*: 'Where is the doll?' No response. 'Go and fetch me the doll.'

You will notice that many of these techniques can help children who don't verbalise readily, by putting more emphasis on comprehension of language rather than forcing them to use language each time to answer direct questions or explain actions. Many children's comprehension skills outrun their expressive fluency, but their ability to explain does improve later.

Note that there is a lot of stress on not just giving the child the answer – this comes out, for instance, in no. 3 above. If an answer does have to be given, we get the child to 'incorporate' it by having them make immediate use of it. So we ask them to find another one, or later on we weave it into the review and get them to *use* the new word or idea.

Summary of the teaching approach

Let's summarise the main purpose of the teaching approach, first for the teacher and then for the pupil.

There are two main ways of looking at the approach from the teacher's point of view. First, it provides a technique that can be used as part of normal teaching, without demanding a complete change of philosophy or routine. What it does demand is a very careful focusing on the individual child and an analysis both before and after the session of what ought to be done and of what has happened, so that systematic planning for future exchanges can be undertaken. Second, it gives teachers the satisfaction of being able to make progress even with pupils who have in the past 'defeated' them. Teachers who have tried out our approach found themselves discovering strengths in pupils they had not suspected – or, more simply, realised that they were getting to know far more about the children in their group.

From the pupils' point of view, our purpose is to help them to become 'self-running'. The child is a natural learner. But that does not mean that they will take responsibility for their own learning without any help. In particular, if they come from a background to which school is not a natural extension, in terms of either social relationships or work habits, they may soon give up and decide that school learning is not for them. But when they discover that success is possible, the whole picture can change dramatically. Not only do they begin to learn in the sessions with the teacher, but this carries over into the rest of school activity. Second, the child learns to see the teacher as a 'facility'. The teacher is someone who knows things, who is interested in working them out and talking about them. The child begins to find that the teacher is a natural person to go to for ideas and help. Finally, the pupil sees the teacher as someone who asks meaningful questions, who helps them to see what they are after and why it is worthwhile. The pupil then sees the teacher as someone who is worthy of trust, someone who is concerned with them as a thinking person. If this comes off, we may be giving the child a start in education that will not 'wash out', in the disappointing way that so many pre-school programmes have been found to do in the past.

An example of the dialogue approach

Let us now look at a full-scale example. At one stage in our research project, we asked all the teachers in our experimental group to work the same session, *cutting an apple*, so as to have a basis for comparing different teachers and children in a similar situation. Each was given the following general advice:

> As part of this week's work, we are asking all our teachers to work a sample session in a similar way to the 'Washing a Doll' one used last term.
>
> If possible, this should be done with a child who has not had the lesson before, but we think here that the child should be one of your less well-functioning ones. [In fact, Nora was a 'well-functioning' child.]
>
> Remember to adjust what you do to the needs of the particular child, and to make as much use as possible of the main principles we have used this and last term. Here is a list of the materials you should provide:
>
> apple, orange, potato, red ball.
> knife, ruler, scissors, spoon.
> milk bottle, plate, small toy cup, colander.

One of the teachers wrote out the following notes for herself:

> Ask Nora if she will come and help me to find out the best way to cut an apple.

Show her an apple, orange, potato, red ball.
Ask her what is the same about them all.
Ask her why apple, orange and potato are same.
Ask her why ball and apple are same.
Show picture of fruit and see if she can find apple and orange.
Show picture of children with balls.
Ask if their balls are different.
Ask why boy is muddy.
Say 'He has finished playing ball. What is he going to do now?'
Review – ask which I said we were going to cut.
Put knife, ruler, scissors and spoon in bag and get N to identify them by touch.
Ask what they are for.
Ask what screw in scissors is for.
Have large scissors and ask how they are different.
Ask her to find one with which to cut apple.
Review.
Ask why we can't cut it on table.
What would happen if we did?
Ask her to choose one of milk bottle, plate, small toy cup, colander, on which to cut apple.
Ask what goes into bottle.
Why?
Is there anything else we have when milk is in bottle?
What would happen to milk if we didn't have a top on?
Ask her to put milk bottle away and put cup in colander and put apple on plate.
Cut it in half.
Cut it in quarters.
Review.

Here is a transcript of the session this teacher worked with Nora. It went on for about 17 minutes. While working through it, you should note how far it seems to exemplify the points made in this chapter as well as any doubts you may have about what the teacher does. If necessary, read it more than once. Then read the comments provided. Don't forget that we cannot convey tones of voice or pauses in this kind of transcript, so that inevitably it may read rather stiltedly at times even when it sounds well on the tape.

T1	There we are.
	Now what have we got here, Nora?
	What's this, what's that?
C1	An orange.
T2	Yes. What else have we got?
C2	A tomato.
T3	Is it?
C3	Um, a ball.
T4	Yes, you feel it.
C4	Um.
T5	Is it a tomato?
C5	A ball.
T6	Yes.
	What else is there?
C6	Apple.
T7	Yes.
	What else is there?
C7	Potato.
T8	Yes, a potato. That's right.
	What's the same about all those.
	Can you see?
C8	That's round.
T9	Umm?
C9	That's round.
T10	Round, yes.
	How about that one?
C10	Umm.
T11	Yes?
C11	That's round.
T12	And?
C12	That's flat.
T13	Yes. But is it round?
C13	No.
T14	It may be.
	But if you cut it,
	if you looked at it that way,
	now it looks round doesn't it?
	Does it? Yes.
	Now what's the same about those two?
C14	They're both round.

T15	Yes, they're both round, and what are they?
C15	An apple and orange.
T16	Yes. Yes. Do you know the name for those?
C16	No.
T17	If you have an apple, oranges and bananas, all together, What's the name for all of them?
C17	Fruit.
T18	Fruit. Yes. Fruit. And what's that, now let's have a look, what's the same about those two?
C18	Round.
T19	Yes, they're both round; there's something else the same about those two, what else is it?
C19	Orange.
T20	No, about those two.
C20	Round.
T21	Yes, they're round. How about the colour.
C21	Red.
T22	Which one's red?
C22	That one red.
T23	Yes, they're both red, aren't they? Yes, that's right. Now, what's the same about those three?
C23	That's round, that's round, that's round, that's round.
T24	Yes, but what can you do to all of them? What do you do to all of them?
C24	You put them in the oven. Peel.
T25	After it has been in the oven what do you do with it?
C25	Eat it.
T26	What do you do with that one?
C26	Peel it.
T27	And then what do you do?
C27	Eat it.
T28	And how about that one?
C28	Eat it with the peel on or take the peel off.
T29	Yes you can, that's a good girl. And how about this one? Can you eat that?

C29	No.
T30	No, that's a good girl.
	I'm going to show you a picture down here.
C30	A greengrocer's shop.
T31	A greengrocer's shop, yes.
	And can you find something in this picture that we have just been looking at?
	What are those?
C31	Oranges.
T32	Oranges?
C32	Yes.
T33	Oranges, yes. What else can you see?
C33	Apples.
T34	Yes. That's what you have just been looking at.
	And in this picture, that I've got over here, there's something else. It's a little bit different, in the picture.
C34	Footballers. Footballs.
T35	Yes.
	Are they different from our ball?
C35	Yes.
T36	Why?
C36	Because they are harder.
T37	Yes.
	And probably they're, what?
	What is a football, it's?
C37	Big.
T38	Big, yes.
	Why do you think he's dirty?
C38	Because he's been playing football.
T39	Yes, he has hasn't he,
	very dirty;
	what does he need to do now; he's finished his game of football,
	what does he need to do?
C39	Wash himself.
T40	Yes,
	what's she been playing?
C40	Football, or bouncy ball.
T41	A bouncy ball,
	but she's not muddy, is she?
	Why isn't she muddy?

C41 Because she's been playing with a bouncy ball.

T42 Yes. Is that ball like our ball?
Does our ball bounce?
Do you want to try it and see if it does?
A ball. Try the ball,
That one's the ball, you try the ball, Nora.
Does it bounce?

C42 No.

T43 No. It doesn't. That's right.
What did I, now let me see, what did we do in the beginning, what did I ask you to come and help me do?
That's right.

C43 Cut a orange.

T44 It wasn't an orange, it was an...?

C44 An apple.

T45 Apple, yes.
So we've looked at the ball; and we've looked at what?
Can you remember what we looked at?
They're underneath my hand.
There was a...?

C45 Orange.

T46 Orange, yes, and...

C46 Apple.

T47 Yes.

C47 And a potato.

T48 Yes.

C48 And a ball.

T48 Yes, good girl.
And we are going to use the...

C49 Apple.

T50 Apple, that's right.
In this bag we've got some other things.
Now can you put your hand in,
that's it, and then, wait a minute,
I don't want you to look, but just feel.
You can put both hands in if you like,
Ah, let's have a look.
Do you know what that is?

C50 A knife.

T51 A knife, yes. Take it out.
Yes. Put it on the table.

	Yes.
	Now, put your hand in again,
	What's that –
C51	Scissors.
T52	Yes. That's it.
	Good girl, take it out.
	Yes. Put your hand in again.
	That's more difficult.
	What do you think it is?
	You might not know what that is.
	Um, you use it to draw lines with, or to measure things with.
C52	Tape measure.
T53	It could be a tape measure,
	but a tape measure's soft, this is . . .
C53	Hard.
T54	It's hard, yes, so what is it?
	It begins with 'r', a r . . .
C54	A ru . . .
T55	A ruler.
C55	Yes.
T56	Have you heard that name before? Ruler.
	Where?
C56	My daddy's got a ruler.
T57	Your daddy's got a ruler.
	There's just one more thing in there, let's see if you can find it.
	You might have to go right down to the bottom of that bag.
	Now, what's that?
C57	A spoon.
T58	A spoon, yes, that's it, good girl.
	Now which do you think we can cut the apple with?
	Yes.
	Why can we cut the apple with that?
C58	Because it's got a shape down there.
T59	Yes, yes. But why?
C59	'Cos it's got a sharp point.
T60	It's got a sharp . . .
C60	Point.
T61	Well, it hasn't got a point, it's got a curve.
	It's got a sharp – what's that bit called,

do you know?

It's called a . . . blade.

C61   Blade.

T62   Blade. Yes.

C62   My daddy does the chips for my dinner . . . sharp knife.

T63   Oh dear.

C63   And he keeps on getting a one what doesn't have a sharp point.

And he doesn't cut his food with it. He just eats with it, with something on his knife.

T64   Yes. Yes. Well, can you see if you can cut the apple with any one of the other things?

Can you cut it with this one, try.

Can you?

If you pressed hard, could you?

You can a little bit, look, can't you.

It's not very good though, is it. Try the ruler.

You can a little bit, can't you.

Try the scissors.

What do we really use scissors for? To cut what?

C64   Paper.

T65   Yes, or what?

C65   Er. Or cotton.

T66   Or cotton, yes. Or, mat . . .

C66   Material.

T67   Material. Yes.

Now let's go and have a look over there.

Can you find the colander on the table?

C67   Yes.

T68   And bring it over to me.

C68   And there's a cup.

T69   Can you bring me the colander over?

No you bring it over to the table.

It's heavy, can you manage it?

Yes. Can you put it on the table?

That's right. Now you come and sit down.

I put the spoon over there.

Can you put the ruler over there, that's it, and the scissors?

Before you put the scissors over there, show it to me.

Now can you tell me what that bit's for, on the scissors?

	Do you know what that bit is there?
	It's a screw.
	Do you know what it's for?
C69	Yes, for screwdriver to work.
T70	Yes, yes, but what's it for with the scissors.
C70	To open it up.
T71	Yes, it's to hold two bits together so that they can cut, they can move.
	Put it over there.
	Now, can you remember what we had?
C71	Yes.
T72	Underneath there.
C72	A ruler and a spoon.
T73	Yes, a ruler and a spoon and . . . ?
C73	Scissors.
T74	Yes, scissors.
	And which one did we find,
	what did we find was best to cut with?
C74	That.
T75	What's that?
C75	Knife.
T76	Yes. Now we are going to find something to put it on.
	Have a look at these.
C76	A plate.
T77	Yes.
C77	To put it on.
T78	Yes. Why choose the plate, what's wrong with that?
C78	'Cos it won't put that on. You can't cut it with that.
	'Cos it's plastic.
T79	Yes, it is plastic, yes,
	what would happen if we, it would go in
	but it is a bit, it would just fit in.
	Won't it.
	But it is a bit difficult, so we put that over there.
	Now what else, what's that?
C79	Bottle.
T80	Yes, what do we use that for?
C80	To roll with, don't we?
T81	Um?
C81	To roll with.
T82	Yes, but what do we put in that?

C82	Milk.
T83	Yes, just like that, or does it have something else?
C83	No.
T84	No? How about something on the top?
	What goes on the top of this milk?
	What would happen if we just put the milk in?
	Without something on the top?
C84	It would all fall out.
T85	Yes, so what do we put on the top?
C85	A milk bottle top.
T86	Yes.
	You put that up there. No, no, can you.
	That would fall off.
	Yes, it will.
	Put that over there then.
	How about this?
C86	This will.
T87	Can you reach?
C87	No.
T88	It's a bit difficult,
	you've got to lift your arms right up, haven't you?
C88	Yes.
T89	Put that up there then.
	So we're going to use the . . . ?
C89	Spoon.
T90	We're going to use the . . . ?
C90	Plate.
T91	Yes. All right then.
	Now can you cut the apple in half, if I help you, if I hold it?
	Is it hard?
C91	Yes.
T92	Is it?
	Careful of your fingers.
	You look what you are doing.
	Shall I help?
C92	Yes.
T93	Now how many bits have you got?
C93	Two bits.
T94	Yes, you've cut it in . . . ?
C94	Half.
T95	In half.
C95	There's pips in there.

T96	That's right, yes.
	Can you cut those two bits in half?
C96	No.
T97	That's it.
C97	Pips came out.
T98	Yes, now that bit.
	Oops.
	Now, how many bits have you got?
C98	Three bits.
T99	You count them again.
C99	One, two, three, four.
T100	Yes. You've cut it into ... quarters.
	You call that cutting it into quarters,
	that's very good.
	Now what did we do in the beginning?
	What did we choose in the beginning to cut?
	Right at the beginning.
	We had an ... ?
C100	Orange.
T101	Orange and a ... ?
C101	Ball.
T102	Yes, and a ... ?
C102	A potato.
T103	And a?
C103	Orange.
T104	We said an orange, and ... ?
C104	Apple.
T105	Apple. And which did we choose?
C105	An apple.
T106	Yes, that's right, good.
	And what else did we look at? To cut with?
C106	Spoon.
T107	There was a spoon and a ... ?
C107	Ruler.
T108	Yes, and ... ?
C108	And a knife.
T109	And a ... something else?
C109	A sieve.
T110	A, no, a ... something to cut with?
	It did cut but we don't usually use it to cut apples with,
	we usually use it to cut paper with?
C110	Scissors.

T111 Scissors, yes. And which one did we choose?
C111 Knife.
T112 That's right.
Now, what were the other things we looked at to put the apple on?
C112 The sieve, the colander.
T113 Yes, the sieve and the colander, and a . . . ?
C113 Bottle.
T114 Yes, and a . . . ?
C114 And a cup.
T115 And which did we choose?
C115 Knife.
T116 Yes.
Then what did we do?
C116 We cut it in quarters.
T117 We cut it in quarters.
Before we cut it in quarters what did we do?
We cut it in . . . ?
C117 In two.
T118 In halves, yes,
and then we cut it in . . . ?
C118 Quarters.
T119 Yes, that's right, we did.
Did we find the best way to cut that apple, do you think!
Yes. Yes, we did.
Thank you Nora.
Would you like to go and have your milk now?
C119 Yes.
T120 Yes, good girl, off you go.

Some general comments

Although this 'lesson' was given by a teacher who by this time was familiar with the approach and generally sympathetic to it, this is obviously a 'demonstration'. It goes on for rather a long time and probably covered too much ground, ranging over a large variety of areas. Yet Nora (a confident child) remained interested throughout and coped well with the situation. In themselves, the preliminary discussion and activities all make sense and are well varied, but it would probably have been better to get on to the main activity – the actual cutting of the apple – rather sooner.

Specific points

Demands
There is a wide range from 'What's this?' (T1) to 'What's the same?'
(T8) to 'Why isn't she muddy?' (T41).

Follow-ups
This is the crucial area. Again, note the variety of strategies the teacher
uses when Nora fails to get the answer. Note how she gets Nora to say
'fruit' by filling out her question from 'Do you know the name?' to 'If
you have . . . ?' (T16–17). Again, when Nora doesn't say 'ruler' she first
gives her the 'r' before offering the rest of the word (T54–55). Having
given that, she establishes the concept before leaving it (T56).
Similarly, with T66: 'Mat . . . ', C66: 'Material'. She also helps the
child check her own statements – for example, C98: 'Three bits', T99:
'You count them again.' She gives the child the word 'quarters' (T100),
but carefully reviews it in her final review.

Sequence
Though there *is* a theme, this is perhaps the weaker aspect of the
session. The teacher is aware of the end-product, but for the child
much of the session probably appears as separate exploratory bits, not
really related together until the end.

Materials
Materials and content were prescribed for this session by the research
team, but the teacher added good ideas of her own – the pictures and
the 'feely bag'.

Checking the response
Note how the teacher gets Nora to try things out – the cutting imple-
ments, for example, and the milk bottle. Also, she doesn't pursue 'My
daddy's got a ruler' (C56), an uncheckable response, though she
accepts it pleasantly.

Activity
The child's activity is frequently evoked, as in the trying-out throughout the session, examining things together, and agian the 'feely bag'.
All through, the child rather than the teacher does the handling and
examining of tools and objects.

Pacing
As recommended earlier, the session starts gently, progressively
increases the demands on the child, then ends with a review of what

has been done and discovered, making rather fewer demands and ending on a positive note. As it is a longish session, this teacher likes to introduce partial reviews (e.g. T43–50: 'What did we do in the beginning . . . ?' down to 'Apple, that's right'). The main review starts of course with T100, 'Now what . . . ?'.

The agreed agenda

We expect the teacher to agree what is going to be done with the child and to work through steadily (but without too much pushing) to the eventual goal. The start doesn't appear on the tape, unfortunately, as the teacher discussed it with Nora before they sat down together, and as we have already said there were rather a lot of side areas explored. But it does all come together at the end. However, even here she might have spent a little time on what the quarter apples were for – that is, on who is going to get them, thus justifying the session's activity in practical terms.

In summary

This is a generally good session, where the teacher uses the technique flexibly and at the right level for the child. It's not 'perfect' dialogue, but no real lesson is perfect. There's rather too much in it and not always quite enough continuing purpose. But the exchanges make sense, the child is learning and the rapport between teacher and child is excellent at both the social and the intellectual level. You should now look through the transcript again, noting in particular the way the teacher handles the demand–answer–follow-up sequence throughout the session. Notice, however, that at this stage the teacher dominates the conversation and the child's role - intellectually, at any rate — is pretty passive and reactive. With more experience the teacher relaxes more and encourages more original conversation from the child: in these circumstances, the child may take over much of the exploration and even initiate the review. But the teacher remains an essential component in helping the child to define the problem, to put solutions into words and to generalise from specific instances.

CHAPTER 6

The Literary-centred Curriculum

Children and books in pre-school settings: provision, use and potential

Almost all the people professionally concerned with early childhood education believe that young children should be introduced to books. There is much debate about the rather different issue of when and how they should be taught to read for themselves, which we do not intend to consider here, but a considerable consensus exists that books should be provided for children to look at, that they should be encouraged to be interested in books, and that listening to stories and looking at picture books are central parts of the early childhood curriculum because they are good in themselves *and* associated with later success in becoming literate. Here we will review, briefly, first the evidence on the links between book use and literacy, then data on the provision of books in pre-school institutions. We will then consider in more detail the use that is made of these books. This will reveal that there is a paradoxical situation: although there is high provision of books, there is a low use rate. An account of a novel approach that can change this, and is our second supplement to the early childhood curriculum, will form the main part of the chapter.

Book use and literacy

It has been clear for a long time that children who read early are almost invariably children whose lives are full of books and activities involving reading and writing. They tend to have acquired much understanding of the task of reading before beginning school – both some of the necessary 'how to do it' understanding and an appreciation of why reading is worth doing. Studies like those of Durkin (1966) and Clark (1976) show that pre-school children whose early interest in reading is met by parental support and experience of reading often become fluent (and intelligent) readers with little or no explicit instruction. How much children are read to, how much they see other people reading, how much and how explicitly written material is used in daily activities like shopping, knowledge of concepts like 'sound', 'word' and 'sentence', are related to rate and efficiency of learning to read. These activities seem to contribute to achieving the necessary insight into the links between written symbol and word meaning: they (and most particularly story reading activities) also help to establish that reading is or can be useful and entertaining, that 'storying' is a way of constructing and communicating meaning.

A substantial proportion of poor readers, on the other hand, lack experience of books and see little use for reading, indeed may completely misunderstand what it is and how to do it, as a study by Hazel Francis (1982) illustrates. Some children, when asked what's in books, think of pictures not text, and cannot say what 'words', 'letters' and 'numbers' are or how they differ. They have little experience of seeing others read, and make little use of readable material in the environment. They may be very vague about such things even after a year or so of schooling, and often vagueness is associated with low interest and low motivation. Children who understand more about reading say they like it and have plans about what they would read next; children with little understanding may dislike or merely tolerate reading, or try to do it to please parent or teacher. In the infant class, they may obediently try to follow the teacher's instructions to draw, copy words, listen to stories and so forth, but be unable to link these pre-reading activities to adult reading and writing. They can be dependent on their peers as models, but even if children who are better readers enjoy the activity, the poorer readers may not understand that they themselves might eventually enjoy it too. Even reading schemes that support meaningful, personally relevant learning can fail to motivate these children because they cannot link the activities of reading and writing to the rest of their understanding. As far as learning a complex and mysterious skill like reading is concerned, children who know nothing about books and reading will have fewer opportunities and less motivation to read than children who are familiar with the pleasurable and problem-solving uses of books.

The findings of the Bristol study of language development carried out by Gordon Wells and his colleagues (Wells, 1981, 1985, 1986) give us some useful evidence on what experiences are relevant to children's learning to read. They studied the language development of more than

100 Bristol children who came from the widest possible range of backgrounds. Recordings were made of the talk that occurred naturally throughout the day while the children were aged between 15 months and 66 months, thus covering the ages from toddler to infant school. Some children developed faster than others, but the Bristol study found that virtually all children, whatever background they came from, could and did use spoken language in the same wide range of ways, though some children's language was much more complex and much more effective at home than it was for the same child in school, a point worth thinking about as we so often use a child's behaviour in school to diagnose how competent they are in other places too. Barbara Tizard, too, has found that many children who seemed to be 'language-delayed' in the classroom were perfectly successful language users at home (Tizard and Hughes, 1984).

As we discussed in earlier chapters, how you talk depends in part on how the other party (or parties) to the conversation talk; most children have developed an adequate use of language for the normal conversations of home and playground by the age of 5. 'Classroom language' is one of the subtly specialised uses of language that not everyone may have mastered to quite the same degree. 'Literature language' may be another specialism. In Wells's study, children differed considerably in how well they got on in the early stages of learning to read and write. One test that predicted their reading attainment particularly well was their 'knowledge of literacy', which was strongly associated with a cluster of items on a questionnaire about the child's experiences which the parents had filled in. These crucial items concerned activities related to literacy: the number of books the child owned, the child's interest in literacy, and his or her interest in activities associated with literacy. There were differences in these items between the middle-class and working-class children, just as there are social class differences in reading, writing and discussing what is read or written, though there are few differences in the language children had shown they could use in speech. Social class differences in 'readiness for school' may have less to do with language differences than they have with differences in activities related to writing and reading.

Such activities take various forms. Hall (1987) reviews the evidence on 'the emergence of literacy'. He compares it with the development of spoken language and its use, which he sees as a matter of child construction within parent facilitation not parent instruction, where oral language is used for non-linguistic ends (including developing meaning and understanding the world, and participating in social interaction).

He argues that literacy, like spoken and heard language, is used to create meanings and to allow communication between people. Many early experiences relevant to literacy are embedded in a social inter-action, for example discussion of a shopping list (Tizard and Hughes, 1984). Such interaction carries information about literacy – for example, that writing can be used to organise information and plan events, that it can be stored and amended, that it can be translated by reading into spoken language – incidental to the social purpose of feeding the family. Hall believes that it may be more powerful intel-lectually, therefore, than 'purer' literacy activities such as reading storybooks. Possibly, he argues, the child could learn about literacy as 'naturally' as he or she learns to talk and to listen.

Children growing up in literate cultures are likely to have a great deal of writing around them in the form of 'environmental print' – shop signs, advertisements, slogans on T-shirts, as well as books, newspapers and letters. Many young children show much interest in this print and make good use of it. Hall argues that such use is an in-trinsic part of becoming literate. It develops along with experience of being read to, which is known to show a high correlation with learning to read well. Parents reading stories may discuss such text-based concepts as 'word' and 'letter' as well as modelling reading behaviour. Stories also provide experience with 'literary language' and with settings beyond the child's daily life: again these can be discussed, and children can reflect on text and experience. The whole constellation of seeing text, being read to, using written and spoken language, and dis-cussion with more expert users, may lead to 'emergent' literacy well before reading and writing are formally taught in school.

When Wells and his colleagues looked at children's reading and writing activities, however, they found that how often the child listened to a story being read or told from a book was much more related to being a relatively early and easy reader than how often the child had looked at books or even talked about pictures in books. Almost all the children in their sample sometimes looked through books, naming objects, colours and so forth in the 'ritual naming game'. The 'ritual naming game' is the sort of sequence often set up by adults looking at pictures (or objects) with a young child. They look at a picture and the adult encourages the child to label it appropriately. The result is dialogue like this (the example is from Gordon Wells's study, but David Wood has similar ones – Wood et al., 1980):

Mother: What's that? [Points to a picture]
Child: House.
Mother: House. That's right: house.
Child: Bump. [This child always says this when he sees a car]
Mother: That's a car. Where's the telephone?
Child: There . . . look.
Mother: That's right.

(Wells, 1985, p. 241)

The adult both asks the question and knows the 'right' answer. The child both answers the question and knows that the adult already knows the answer. It is perhaps a precursor of the sorts of 'display' questions very often asked in schools. Wells believes that this sort of activity is useful for early vocabulary development (though not necessarily *more* useful for vocabulary than stories are) but later on may be counterproductive if it leads the child to believe that books are mainly for providing material that adults ask display questions about and children just have to label. Sometimes looking at pictures did lead to extended discussions, but this was far more likely to occur if the pictures were linked to a story.

Wells argues that stories have a central role in learning, indeed that the activity of learning or discovery is one of making things meaningful, constructing stories in the mind and sharing one's interpretation of events and ideas with others. In this book, for example, we have been telling a story (one we believe to be true) about how young children can be helped to learn, and we hope that the characters, motives and actions ring true enough with our readers for them to adopt some of our story into their own mental model and their own practice of early education. Stories convey information, ranging from the myths that try to explain the basic beliefs of the culture to the anecdotes that illustrate our own stories of our day-to-day selves. They allow us to be spectators instead of participants totally concerned with getting things done, so that reflection, comment and other meta-cognitive activities become possible. They allow us to profit from other people's experience, as well as reflecting on our own. Vicariously, through listening to their stories, we can understand more about the plight of the ill-treated stepchild Cinderella or the Cowardly Lion who cannot live up to the expected norm of bravery, or share in triumphs that will never otherwise be our own, such as John Keats encapsulates in his sonnet 'On first looking into Chapman's Homer', when the clarity of the translation makes Keats feel a full understanding of Homer's heroes *and* of the excitement of discovery such as is felt by an astronomer first finding a new planet, or a discoverer first seeing a new ocean – to take an example from a different area of literature!

Script theory, indeed, as we described in Chapter 4, suggests that we use our own 'scripts' or stories to make sense of all our experiences, because we rarely have *all* the sensory information that would tell us without any ambiguity what we are experiencing. From infancy onwards we are constructing stories about the regularly occurring events we take part in – having dinner, going shopping, what to wear when the weather's hot or cold or wet, and so forth. Other people offer us their own stories about such events as well as about those that occur more rarely. Linking rare or notable events to everyday analogies is one of the functions of the stories adults tell children. We know from some recent research that mothers who do this a lot, setting up 'world links' between the present event and a similar event elsewhere, or the general principles that underlie both, have children whose development of cognition and language, and later school competence, is particularly advanced (Meadows, Mills and Puckering, 1987). Sharing stories enriches our perhaps less dramatic reality; they are one of the tools we have for making sense of the world.

Using stories, Wells says, means using words to *create* a world as well as to *fit* the world. The words of the story provide the context in which the text itself, and the knowledge it conjures up, can be understood. Stories thus require full attention to linguistic meaning, to the beginnings of what Margaret Donaldson (1978) called 'disembedded knowledge'. This sort of attention and this sort of knowledge will be required in the classroom. Eventually, whatever the curriculum area, children will need to follow and to construct for themselves 'stories' incorporating the relevant factors, suggesting causes and consequences, considering human emotions and motives. As well as narration and description, the classroom requires dealing with curriculum content that can only be presented as stories; however much we may wish to give learners concrete experience, there are limits to how far we can introduce weddings, volcanoes, Victorians, sub-atomic particles and dinosaurs into the school. They have to be dealt with through language, that is, through some sort of 'story'.

Listening to a story being read also gives children quite a good opportunity to gather useful experience of text. They may see the reader attending carefully to those mysterious black squiggles, even occasionally pointing to them. They may notice that some of the squiggles resemble the writing seen in other contexts, writing on objects seen in street or shop or the 'writing' they themselves sometimes do. Even more than this, listening to stories lets the child learn that the story is there in the text. Every time the story is read, whoever the reader may be, the words are the same, the page is turned at the same point in the plot to reveal the same next bit, the story is (literally) in the book, not like ordinary talk in the reader's or speaker's head. The context for understanding it does not have to be created from outside.

The language of stories is also somewhat different from the ordinary day-to-day language of conversation: probably more formal, probably grammatically tidier, probably using different ways of linking the present comment to past ones. Experience of the sort of language that stories use will be useful to the beginning reader starting to decipher them.

It is also the case that stories give rich opportunities for sustained discussion between reader and listener. In Wells's study it was the parents who read most to their children who were most likely to get involved in discussing a particular story or particular episode at length, and it was these children who were most likely to do well at reading in school. Listening to stories lets the child's world stretch beyond his or her own experiences into imaginary worlds whose inhabitants have different experiences, different feelings, different knowledge. Discussing these worlds allows the child to learn about them *and* to reflect on how the real world compares with the imaginary one: it is a way of learning about, and coming to terms with, reality. Reading and writing seem to be particularly conducive to searching for general principles to try to explain particular events – a habit that is much in demand in later education, and is an important component of what we mean by intelligence.

Finally, parents who read a lot to their children commonly do so because they enjoy reading for themselves and they are skilled readers. Given this, they can put on a splendid performance which both they and the children enjoy, and which the child can summon up in imagination when looking at the story book alone, or when engaged in imaginative play. Where parents do not enjoy reading, the child is likely to get a less enjoyable performance less often, and will lack both experience of books and a model of reading being a rewarding activity. Such a child may lack both knowledge and motivation when faced with the task of learning to read.

It seems possible, then, that mastery of the beginnings of literacy is one of the major determinants of early educational achievement. It is more important than social class *per se*, though social class can function as a rough indicator because there are self-perpetuating differences in literacy associated with social class. Literacy vies with 'intelligence' as a predictor: whether the two are separable, and how they influence each other, are not questions we can usefully discuss here, except to point out that as educators we may like to focus on literacy, which we know we can influence. Further, it is better than 'possible' that listening to stories is an excellent facilitator of understanding literacy. Stories enable children to relate their own experience to that of others. Creating and interpreting and sharing stories sustains and enriches their attempts to make sense of their own worlds. It also shows them how important language is as a means of representing thoughts, feelings and experience, of organising and communicating them, perhaps more eloquently and more permanently than ordinary conversation can do. Having these sorts of understandings, children are better placed to begin to master reading and writing, as they must do if they are to succeed in school.

The provision of books in pre-school institutions and their use

Given evidence like this about the importance of books and reading, it is hardly surprising that almost all pre-school centres and infant school classes provide book corners and story times for their children. The Child Health and Education Study (CHES) made a survey (van der Eyken *et al.*, 1984) of all the pre-school centres in England and Wales, which included questionnaire items on what materials and activities were provided and how often – 95 per cent of playgroups, 99 per cent of nursery classes and 99 per cent of nursery schools provided a book corner for 'most' or 'all' sessions. Nearly as many (respectively 86 per cent, 92 per cent and 89 per cent) had a story-reading to the whole group 'most' or 'all' sessions. Books were the most commonly provided of all materials in this survey and indeed a great many pre-school institutions were using reading kits and reading schemes. All the observational studies of pre-school centres that we mentioned in Chapter 3 confirm that book corners and story times are very common indeed – an important part of normal 'good practice'.

'Practice' may not be quite the right word, however, since the research evidence is in complete agreement that the books so universally provided are universally little used. Pre-school children in Avon, Hertfordshire, London, Oxfordshire, Dunbartonshire and Stoke-on-

Trent, for example, all made very little spontaneous use of the book corners provided in their nursery class or school or playgroup.

Kathy Sylva and her colleagues (1980) observed Oxfordshire pre-school centres. They saw seventy-eight bouts of activities connected with the 3Rs (0.6 per cent of all bouts). Almost all were in nursery schools. For almost all bouts the children involved seemed to be highly absorbed, and the average duration of a bout was just under 4 minutes. It is not clear how many 3Rs activities were reading rather than 'riting or 'rithmetic; nor is it clear how many of the more frequent activity 'examination' (1.5 per cent of bouts) involved looking at books. It is clear, however, that book use was associated with a fairly high level of cognitive demands, that it 'stretched' children and interested them, but that it was a fairly rare occurrence.

Sheila Mably (1977), observing her own Hertfordshire nursery class, saw in a term only three occasions on which a child spontaneously chose to work at a book. One involved two moderately interested children and lasted 2 minutes. The other two bouts, by the same child, totalled $2\frac{1}{2}$ minutes and involved the child alone, though at the end of one bout the child did approach an adult with the request 'please read me this book'. The response was 'I can't now, I will at story time', and the child went and put the book away.

Ruth Burberry (1980) observed all ten playgroups in a suburb of Bristol. All provided book corners (and story sessions) but books were the least used of all materials. A large proportion of children *never* went into the book corner. Those who did go in spent only a short time there, usually alone, and cognitively complex behaviour was not conspicuous. She summarises how the book corner was used as follows:

> Typically the 'activity' consisted of the child wandering into the book corner, taking a book from the display unit, sitting down, flicking through the pages (a few children did talk to themselves), replacing the book and wandering out. This could be completed in less than half a minute!
>
> (Burberry, 1980, p. 67)

On three occasions in these playgroups an adult sat in the book corner and read to small groups of children.

> The presence of an adult in the book corner had a marked effect upon the length of time spent [there] by the children . . . It was also observable that the presence of an adult and a small group of children in the book corner had a

magnetic effect in drawing children away from other activities.

(Burberry, 1980, p. 68)

We and our colleagues observed twenty classes in Outer London
nursery schools, and 320 focal children within them, during free
sessions (Meadows and Cashdan, 1983). The focal children's activities
were recorded through nearly 3,000 bouts of activity. A total of 3 per
cent of all bouts involved the use of books. These bouts were typically
brief and repetitive, just glancing through the pictures or part of the
book, and did not make full use of books, though the children showed
a high degree of interest in their activity. Again, adult participation
prolonged the use of books, but adult participation was less common
here than with art and craft activities. The normal use of books seemed
to be as a brief relaxation after more demanding activities.

This study also involved observations focused on teachers throughout the school day, and thus provides data on behaviour during about
360 story sessions. The main information is on teacher language and
child response. As might be expected, the frequency of teacher utterances that involved giving simple information – in this case comments
on things in the story or its pictures – increased significantly, but so did
managerial directions such as 'pay attention', 'sit down or the children
behind won't be able to see'. Children's responses were often coded as
inappropriate, which would seem to suggest that the children were not
absorbed by the story. Story sessions were generally brief, though not
as short as those in Ruth Burberry's observations of playgroups,
which lasted only about 5 minutes: stories read were always brief
picture books.

These very consistent results suggest that the use made of books in
pre-school centres is not giving children much experience of the uses
(or delights) of literacy. Although almost all pre-school centres
provide books, very few children use them, and almost all their use
involves brief 'glancing through'. During story sessions, teachers have
to spend a lot of time managing the group and children often do not
seem to be very much interested in the story. Where the story is discussed, comments are simple and 'one off', questions are mainly
managerial or display questions. Books and story are isolated and not
particularly rewarding events.

Two questions arise: first, does it matter, and, second, is it inevitable
that book use in the pre-school should be infrequent, brief and unin-
spiring? The answer to the first question obviously depends on value

judgements about the importance of encouraging interest in literacy and about the pre-school curriculum. We have put the case for literacy and book use in the earlier part of this chapter. It is, however, worth pointing out that we cannot rely on children being read to at home: the CHES data on 5 year olds reveal that 12 per cent had not been read to *at all* in the previous week, and a further 30 per cent had been read to on three or fewer days. It is also worth remembering that the primary school curriculum places a heavy emphasis on reading. Our own value judgements about the question lead us to the answer, yes, it does matter that children's experience of books in pre-school centres should be rewarding. If it *can* be made so, it *should* be.

In what follows we are going to describe the work of Christianne Hayward, which demonstrates the value of a pre-school curriculum that gives a far more important place to books than was seen in the studies we have mentioned so far. It shows that the answer to our second question can quite easily be 'No'.

Literary theme development in the nursery classroom

Christianne Hayward is a Canadian nursery school teacher who, loving books herself, devised a nursery curriculum that centres on developing a literary theme. She worked with Sara Meadows in Bristol in the early 1980s, evaluating the effect of her curriculum on how children used books and developed as potential readers. This account of her approach is drawn from the M.Ed thesis (1982b) which describes this research evaluation. Christianne has been continuing her work since in Canada, and some of the teachers she worked with in Bristol are also using literary themes as a core in their classrooms.

Literary theme development is very different from the provision and use of books observed in most pre-school groups, where a collection of books is made available throughout the session but deliberately isolated from other activities in a 'quiet corner', and a short story is read in a separate timetable slot each day, usually at the end of the session. This segregation of books can put them, as we have seen, at the periphery of the nursery curriculum. All too often books are associated with passiveness and quiet; children are expected to be more or less silent and immobile listeners except when the teacher asks the group a question. The book corner is frequently used as a place to put a distressed child (or one who is distressing other children) until they have 'calmed down'! As we have seen, under this system the children make little spontaneous use of books, and story times can leave a lot of children quite uninterested. Literary theme development really does change all this – to a degree that surprised our best hopes as we evaluated it – and it seems to have a strong effect on children's interest in books outside the classroom.

Christianne Hayward's innovation centres on choosing a book of some substance rather than a short story, and reading it as a serial over a period of two–four weeks. During this time, the usual classroom activities – art, construction, role play, science and so forth, and the other books in the book corner – focus on ideas and material related to the theme of the book being read. For example, one book she used in her research study with a class of 3–5 year olds in a disadvantaged area of Bristol was Richard Adams' *Watership Down*. She part read, part told the story as a three-week serial, using the book of pictures from the cartoon film version as illustration. During the reading, the story characters appeared in jigsaw puzzles and table games, a real rabbit lived in a hutch in the 'animal corner', rafts were sailed on the water trough and burrows dug in the sand tray, and the area that had been a Wendy House was transformed under the children's instructions into a green hill with a burrow under it. These options were extremely attractive to the children, many of whom spent much of their time 're-reading' and living out the story, enacting favourite incidents, getting their parents to read the book to them at home, and generally showing a greatly increased interest in both school and books. In formal testing at the end of the evaluation, they showed more knowledge of the concepts that are necessary for beginning to read, and enhanced vocabulary which they used outside the classroom, away from *Watership Down* itself. Discussing the story, acting it out, predicting what might happen next and referring back to earlier incidents were activities that developed rapidly and extremely richly, and gave rise to improvements in social development as well as in language and the beginnings of literacy. The same sort of interest and achievement was to be seen with the other stories used, and it spread to books in general.

Here is an example of the sort of play and discussion that the literary theme produced. It is chosen because it is a typical record of 10 minutes of play, not because it was more exciting than usual. Vicky and Kenny are playing in the Watership Down corner where there is a 'hill' of beanbags covered with a green sheet and a 'burrow' big enough for the children to crawl through and sit in, made from a wire spiral again covered with cloth. The walls and screen separating the area from the rest of the classroom are covered with blue paper for sky and green for grass, and decorated with a few plastic daffodils. A range of rabbit glove puppets hang on hooks on the screen: the class have previously insisted that there should be a puppet for each favourite character. Sara Meadows, on one of her visits to the class, is sitting at a table just outside the area. Christianne Hayward is lurking behind the screen recording what the children do, unknown to both them and Sara!

When the record begins Vicky and Kenny are inside the tunnel, whispering about Fiver. Vicky emerges from the tunnel and jumps on the hill. Kenny rolls in the tunnel with the Bigwig glove puppet on his hand, and says to Vicky 'I'm Mr Bigwig'. Vicky replies, pointing out a felt carrot, 'This is it'. They both look at the carrot. Vicky has the Kehaar puppet on one hand and the Clover puppet on the other. She is still jumping up and down. Kenny says: 'Hey Kehaar! Let us have Kehaar.' Vicky gives him the puppet, but also puts forward the Clover puppet, saying 'Have to take care of Clover though'.

Kenny comes up to Sara Meadows and shows her the Bigwig puppet, while Vicky watches. He says: 'I'm Bigwig. I'm bad.' Sara: 'Why? Do you mean sick bad or naughty bad?' Kenny: 'Sick bad. 'Cause Hazel's not the leader. Hazel has been shot.' Sara: 'Who by?' Kenny and Vicky, both talking at once, explain that the farmer shot the rabbit. They back up each other's comments, telling what happened accurately but too fast to record. Kenny finishes by saying 'Hazel's not really dead'.

Sara: 'Where is he now?'

Vicky: 'He's home now.'

Sara: 'Oh good, that's where he should be resting.'

Vicky says, 'I'm Kehaar, I slapped him', illustrating the slap with the glove puppet's wing.

Sara: 'You didn't slap Hazel?'

Vicky: 'No, Bigwig, 'cause he asked if my wing was better. Would you like to hear what he said when he came back?'

Sara: 'What did he say?'

Vicky: 'He went "perfect landing"', role playing Kehaar's landing just as awkwardly as in the book.

Vicky: 'When Hazel said "Are you still bad?" he went "Perfect landing. Perfect landing". Then he spat out black things from Hazel. It's nice to be back.'

Vicky continues to discuss the connection between Kehaar and Bigwig. She mentions splashing the patient with fresh water, and mimes this at Sara.

Sara: 'Oh, that's nice. Very refreshing. Does it have a nice smell?'

Vicky: 'It smells like, um, daffodils.'

Sara: 'I don't think I've ever smelled daffodils – that's lovely.'

Meanwhile Kenny has moved back into the Watership Down corner, saying to Vicky and Sara, 'I can roll on top of the burrow. Like this, see. Bigwig can roll on top . . . I'm going to be Blackberry.' After a minute he comes back to Vicky and Sara; Vicky is still expounding the story.

Vicky: 'Bigwig makes sure Kehaar is taken care of. Carries things for Kehaar till his wing gets better.'

Vicky and Kenny tell about things which are brought to Kehaar, and how he can't carry anything.

Kenny: 'I'm feelin' poorly,' showing how the glove puppet's wig is coming unstuck from its head.

Sara: 'Why?'

Kenny: ''Cause my friend is dead.'

Vicky is continuing a monologue in Kehaar's strange accent and says 'Perfect well, perfect well.'

Figure 6.1   *Average percentage of children recorded using the book corner per day in any given week*

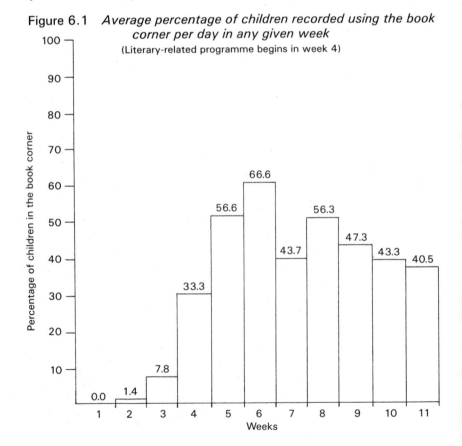

(Literary-related programme begins in week 4)

Many such episodes of play enlivened the classroom during the literary theme programme, so that everyone who saw it was struck by how much the children were enjoying it. In order to evaluate the curriculum more formally, Christianne Hayward measured various aspects of children's classroom behaviour before and during the time that first *Watership Down* and then *The Wizard of Oz* were being told. The first, crude, measure taken was how much children used the book corner. Before the literary programme started, children very rarely spontaneously looked at books outside story time; in all there were three occasions of using the book corner in three weeks, two occasions when a solitary child wandered in and, quickly, out, and one occasion when a group of children gathered around a nursery nurse who was stationed there to read. Thus initial usage was at the same low level as in the London, Oxfordshire and Avon studies. Once the literary programme started, use shot up, and remained high: at least 40 per cent of the children in the class were seen using the book corner *each day* after the first week. As Figure 6.1 shows, the level of book use was much higher after *Watership Down* was started in the fourth week. Every single child in the class increased book use.

Christianne and the other staff in the nursery noted down what the children did once they were in the book corner. Figures 6.2 and 6.3 illustrate what happened. The children looked at more books, the average being over sixteen books in one afternoon's observation by the middle of the programme. Often a small group of children looked at the same book together, sharing its content. The current serial and books related to its theme were particularly likely to be shared in this way. Children 'read' these books together, looking at the pictures, reviewing what they had heard in earlier storytellings, predicting what might happen next, discussing characters or using the book to prove a point to another child or to check something. Children showed a lot of practical knowledge about books, involvement in the story, and interest in concepts that are very complex, as the following examples show.

| 5th February | Chris and Lizzy are flipping through the W/D book when Chris exclaims: 'There he is again, look, the one without an eye. I'm going ahead to see what happens next.' |
| 17th February | Four children form a nucleus around a visitor with the W/D book. They went through the book page by page, telling her |

the story, sometimes supporting each other and at other times interrupting. They ventured their own predictions for the conclusion of the story and warned the visitor of the various 'danger bits'. In exciting parts they virtually acted out the story.

2nd March   Kenny sought out Peter and opened the W/D book to where the Black Rabbit heads off towards Hazel... 'Is that what Fiver sees in the future?'

4th March   Vicky was looking through one of the books in the book corner when she stopped, pointed to a letter 'W' and said, 'That's what Watership Down begins with!' Then, she picked out the letter 'B' and said 'Bigwig and Blackberry begin with that letter.'

A similar 'before and after' analysis of the children's spontaneous play was made, using versions of the scales developed in the Open University study which we described in Chapter 3. All the eight

Figure 6.2   *Average number of books used per day in any given week*

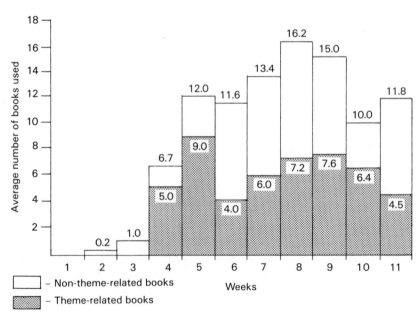

    ☐ – Non-theme-related books

    ▦ – Theme-related books

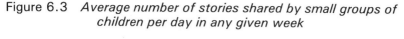

Figure 6.3 *Average number of stories shared by small groups of children per day in any given week*

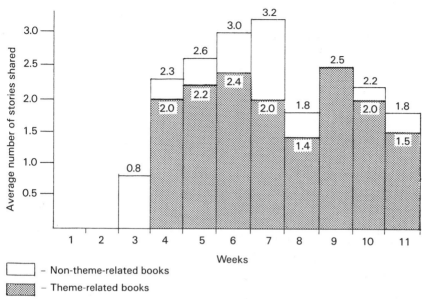

☐ – Non-theme-related books

▨ – Theme-related books

children who were observed in detail showed significant changes for the better in several aspects of their behaviour. At the 'before' stage they were very much like the children seen in the other studies of the ordinary free play classroom; by the 'after' stage their play had become much better developed. They were much more likely to be very involved in their play, much less likely to show low involvement. They spent less time — one-tenth of the 'before' level – wandering vaguely about or listlessly flitting from activity to activity. They were more likely to play co-operatively with other children. They talked more with them. They spent rather longer with their activities. They used a great deal more language that used the literary theme's vocabulary or drew analogies with the story.

These changes were particularly great when the play activity was related to the literary theme. The children preferred material related to the current literary theme for every nursery classroom activity except painting, where perhaps they felt they could not satisfactorily match up to the expert pictures in their story books. In activities such as imaginative play, puzzles and writing they almost always chose the ideas and material of *Watership Down* or *The Wizard of Oz*. The preference was particularly strong when they were role playing. The conventional Wendy House was deserted, and all the stereotyped domestic 'mothers and fathers' games were replaced by re-enactments and extensions of the story. The children often experimented with story concepts in their imaginative play and seemed to enjoy testing out alternative settings with different solutions. They also made many meaningful and deliberate adaptations to the play setting, for example asking for puppets that hadn't originally been provided, or first asking for the Yellow Brick Road to be made into a circle, and then when a gap remained because there was not enough material, adjusting their play and the song that accompanied it accordingly – 'Follow the Yellow Brick Road – and jump over the ditch'! Similarly they used their knowledge of the characters to establish social rules that organised their games, and also manipulated character traits to suit their play sequence: favourite characters and favourite episodes emerged, for example Kenny's enthusiasm for the strong and brave rabbit, Bigwig, and various children's delight in the funny accent of the seagull, Kehaar.

Teacher, nursery nurse, Christianne Hayward and the children's parents all kept notes of occasions when the children showed a particularly interesting reaction to the stories they were hearing. Some of these suggest that the literary emphasis programme had very positive effects for many aspects of the children's development. They retold the story at home, and borrowed the school's copy or searched the book out in the local public library, so that the family was kept abreast of the school's serial and could share the book. Their vocabularies were enhanced. They could draw parallels between the story and real life, distinguishing between fiction and reality. For example, Peter was looking at *The Wizard of Oz* with the teacher. These are his comments: 'Here, the witch, ooh that's where she gets covered with water. If you'd throw a bucket of water at me, I won't melt – my Mum said!' Alternatively, here is a parent's note: 'We saw a black cat this morning – Vicky said, "It's not a cat – it's the Black Rabbit from *Watership Down*. The one who told Hazel to take his skin off so he could go to heaven"'. Finally, Jerry, aged 3, looks in the budgie's cage: 'He's just like Kehaar, and he needs feeding too.' There were even analogies between story and story, for example when Annie said of General Woundwort (a villainous rabbit in *Watership Down*): 'He's strong, but a Kalidah [monster from *The Wizard of Oz*] could rip him in two.' They identified with story characters – Kenny with his hero Bigwig, Vicky with the beautiful rabbit Clover.

Discussing the books was a way into social interaction for some of the younger children, and enacting roles or episodes from them produced more co-operative and elaborated play. The children wanted really good facilities for their imaginative play, and Christianne and her colleagues had to make more and more puppets and add more and more detail to the imaginative centre.

> 20th February Peter decided the Watership Down Centre needed to be organised. 'The burrow has got to have its front on the *down*.' He also thought it should be made permanent. His suggestion of 'blu tack' was shunned by Kenny who thought bricks would be better. Indignant, Peter retorted 'No ways – if it rolls we could be in *real danger*!' Changes and improvements continued to be suggested (some by other children) and then discussed.

The literary theme development curriculum is not intended as a way to teach children to read. Books like *Watership Down*, *The Wizard of Oz*, *Heidi*, *Stig of the Dump*, *Charlotte's Web* and others that have been used are longer and more complex in their language than 'early readers', as well as having much more conceptual range and literary richness. No one would expect a 4 year old to read them in the sense of decoding from symbol to sound and meaning. However, we argued in the first part of this chapter that knowing about books and feeling enthusiastic about stories is one of the major components of becoming a reader. If this is so, the literary theme curriculum might help young children in their preparation for reading, even, perhaps, in their reading itself. As part of evaluating it, we looked to see if there were any effects on 'beginning reading'.

Eight 'focal' children, between $4\frac{1}{2}$ and 5, who had taken part in the literary theme activities were compared with eight children of the same age from each of two other classes in the same school. One test we used was Marie Clay's 'Concepts about Print' test (Clay, 1979). This gives a score indicating the child's status in the age group 5–7: its contents include knowing where the book starts, understanding that the story is in the print rather than in the pictures, reading the text from left to right and top to bottom, and noticing changes in word order and letter order. The eight focal children were significantly better scorers than their peers from the other classes; they scored at above the 6-year-old level on several items, that is, they were more than a year ahead of the average for their age. The Clay test does not show that they were or would be good readers. But it does show that they had very advanced concepts about print and might therefore be particularly well equipped to start reading.

A second way of assessing the children's preparation for reading was to investigate their attitudes to reading as an activity. They were shown a series of eighteen photographs in which children were looking at books, being read to by a parent or teacher, choosing a book in the library, and so forth. They were asked to say whether, if they were doing what was in the picture, they would feel happy, sad or neither, by pointing at faces with the appropriate expression drawn under the photograph. The average 'happiness' score was higher for the 'focal' group than for the other children: seven of the eight said all or all but one of the pictured situations would make them feel happy, a fairly strong indication that they had positive attitudes to books. Six of the sixteen control group children also had this level of generalised positive attitudes, but seven reacted negatively to at least seven pictures, one child saying that every single pictured situation would make him feel unhappy, and several making negative comments about the activity of reading – 'I don't *have* to read books yet', 'I don't want Mummy to read me a book', 'No, I don't like reading except at home', 'No, 'cause every time I looks at them the teacher tells me to read them'. Again, the literary theme programme seems to have had a more desirable effect than the ordinary free play curriculum or the early reading schemes that were being used in one of the control classrooms.

Our final way of making a formal assessment of the impact of the programme on the children was to use a semi-structured story-retelling task. This produced useful samples of the children's ability to use language at length to express themselves. The children were asked to tell Christianne Hayward the story of their favourite book as they remembered it, using the pictures. The tapes were then examined to discover whether the focal children used more different words or more rare words, and whether their retellings included more story material or a different awareness of the story. On all these measures the focal children were indeed significantly ahead of the control group. The control group used mainly very common words and repeated words more than the focal group did; the focal group used more rare words, especially words drawn from the literary theme books, as one would have expected given the evidence from observations that they used their new vocabulary outside the story context. Parents recorded many examples of vocabulary knowledge and story discussion.

Vicky (parent) – 26th March
'Vicky told us all about the *"cyclone"* today that lifted up Dorothy's house.'

Vicky (parent) – 1st April
'When reading *The Great Hamster Hunt* she understood the word *"nocturnal"* – said she knew it from *Watership Down*.'

Chris (mother) – 3rd February
'I caught Chris discussing W/D with his sister again today and he even dominated the dinner conversation. It's amazing – he gave details of W/D, saying the story was getting very *"dangerous"* because a fox was chasing the rabbits. He was asking us if we had any ideas about how to make a burrow in the classroom.'

Chris (mother) – 20th February
'Chris is very talkative today! He said that they heard a lot of W/D as they will be on holiday next week. He said that 'Ke-ara'? is getting very fed up with Bigwig because he is going to steal some does, escaping in a boat. Blackberry is going to test the boat to make sure it sails as he is the one with the brains! Can't keep him quiet tonight; he has told us almost the whole story so far. Can't believe it!'

Most of what the control group said in 'telling the story' was isolated descriptions, and they also made quite a lot of inappropriate statements. The focal group made almost no inappropriate statements and more often anticipated or recalled events, explained causes or drew analogies between the story and 'real life'. They showed much more awareness of the underlying structure of the story and much more often took on the role of 'story-teller'.

Here, as examples, are two complete retellings from the control group and the beginnings of two retellings from the children who had participated in the literary emphasis programme. Despite the fact that all four children chose what book to retell, the difference between the groups is obvious. Vicky's account is particularly impressive.

Control child L: Where The Wild Things Are
- Where The Wild Things Are! Hmm!
- Max banging a branch on his wall. Teddy's tied up! Then he's safe, then he don't drop.

- He is trying to catch the dog.
- His Mom sent him to bed.
- The bed got branches on it (laughs).
- Where's his bed gone to? Stars still there. There's his bed (points to it).
- Where the wild things are now.
- A boat.
- It's a wild thing.
- It's a baby. Look! Stop!
- The wild things. He's King of the wild things. He's going now.
- And there's his supper.
- I bet he was aleep. He was anyway. He was dreaming. His wolf suit is really a sleeping suit.

Control child M: Peter's Chair
- Peter's getting a crocodile.
- The crocodile felled down and the dog runs.
- He's just peeping around and the dog is peeping around and the Mom's putting the dolly, the baby in the pram.
- Peter's Dad painting the chair.
- He's peeping around the chair.
- Peter's taking the chair and the dog's running after Peter.
- The dog's looking at Peter.
- He looks at the cat and Peter looks at the chair.
- The dog sees the baby. He sits on a chair.
- The dog walks away. Peter gets off the chair.
- Peter's hiding behind the curtains.
- He's there, but his shoes are there.
- Peter goes to his Dad and Mom and looks at the baby.
- Peter's painting the chair and the Dad's painting the chair.

Annie (focal child): Watership Down
- I don't want to start at the beginning! I'll show you where I wanna start. (Flips through and stops at page 27.)
- There they crossing 'cause of the dog. Pipkin and Fiver is getting pushed 'cause they're small and it tipped up and they pulled themselves out of the water.
- And Blackberry said – he said it was a good idea and it might come in handy again.
- And they went to the churchyard and Blackberry was tired. The rats are going to attack Bigwig (page 33 – before the relevant

frame). One got his ear and Bigwig swung him round. Kehaar's going to help them.

- He said that there was plenty of room in his burrow. Cowslip's burrow. It was raining so they crept in.
- Fiver thought it smelled funny, didn't he? Pipkin (that's him). Pipkin thought the rabbits looked sick.
- Fiver thinks there was danger and he runned out and Bigwig started yelling at him but he's going to be sorry.
- He give a cry. He got caught in it but they get the peg out, and they all thought Bigwig was dead with it round his neck.
- He gets up though and says: 'Why you going without me?'
- Them's the downs.
- Hazel and Pipkin are going to get some does. That's Nuthanger Farm – they're going to get some does so they can get married.
- That's my favourite one – Clover. They's enemies of the farm; there's a dog and a cat.
- But them rabbits won't get the does – the man comes. They belongs to the man.
- He's going to shine the torch on one of them so they couldn't move. They couldn't move because it gets them in the eyes and they gets frightened.
- He's shot Hazel, the other is waiting for him. He's gone down there. He's gone down the drainpipe.
- He's the black rabbit to take Hazel to heaven. I forgets his name.

Vicky (focal child): Watership Down
- (Pointing to left side of first page). That says *Watership Down* now! This is Watership Down. Hazel and Fiver are going to live there and they went out once and they went looking for some ahh, ahh cowslips, and then Fiver find it and one of the chief rabbits put their paw on it, and then they were both looking sad and Fiver could see that there was something going wrong. He could see that something was going to happen. He thought (pointing to page 9) that was blood but it's really only the sunshine and he said: 'No,' Fiver said to Hazel: 'There's going to be some trouble.' And ahh Fiver, no, Hazel went to Bigwig and they said what Fiver said to Hazel and he went to the chief rabbit and he said he wouldn't go. Ahh, then all the rabbits went and they saw a shadow (page 16 – before the relevant frame) and it was Bigwig. And then Bigwig decided to go and then they was all scared of going through the woods. And then Fiver saw that there was something else going to

happen and he saw a big wing, and then they saw some water and they smelt it. And then Bigwig saw a dog in the forest.

- Yeah, and he found a raft just nearby and Bigwig had to swim. Hazel and Bigwig had to push Fiver and ahh . . . oh Pipkin, and they saw a bird and they nearly pushed up the thing and the two little ones nearly fell off, and then Hazel try to make a path to go and then they went asleep and Hazel and Bigwig went asleep, and then they was going through the church. It was dark and there were some rats they saw (page 33 – before the relevant frame).
- Yeah, they bit Bigwig's ear, and they tried to catch him but they couldn't, and then an owl he come and frighten them all away except for the rabbits . . .
- Then they finded the way out, then it started to rain in the night. They had to find a tree to go under and then a rabbit came out of a hole and he's sort of sick and the rabbit said they they could go in and stay (page 40 – before the relevant frame). And then they find out where all the baby rabbits and the mummy rabbits have been scared – snared, snared.
- Yeah, some of them have been snared. And then Fiver, ahh Fiver thought that up and then Fiver said that there was going to be some more trouble, and then Bigwig started to run off and he got snared (page 67 – before the relevant frame).
- He got snared and he was starting to die and they called two of the rabbits to get the peg and try and get it out. They thought he died and he didn't die. They thought he was dying so they went off. They went on and he woke up and he said: 'Hey, don't go without me.'

Christianne Hayward outlines her way of using a book to integrate the activities of the nursery in her thesis. The first step is choosing the book! She suggests it should have a strong plot with plenty of action, though a story 'form' such as fairy tales or legends, or poetry, can also be used. It is important that the teacher should like the book, since he or she is going to be reading it over several days, and the listeners will certainly pick up signs of the reader's enthusiasm (or lack of it). The children's reactions should also be sensitively considered – the ideal book would challenge and stretch them, but not further than they can reach. They will have different likes and dislikes, even when they are so young. The children focused on in the evaluation study showed a fairly consistent enjoyment of books about animals, and preferred stories that were fairly complex, certainly not 'beginner readers'. However, apart from these two tendencies, individual children had different preferences as to subject matter, style, length and type of illustration – just as adults do.

In order to use material effectively in the classroom, the teacher has to know it well. In literary theme development, this means being thoroughly familiar with the story and being aware of the areas and questions it could potentially be linked to. Familiarity with the story is needed at several different levels. One is vocabulary: the reader needs to be confident about the pronunciation and meaning of unusual words. Young children generally enjoy acquiring new words, so there is no need to take out 'long words' and replace them with items of basic vocabulary as the early stages of reading schemes do, but it *is* necessary to let the children know what these new and strange words mean. Good writers do this: for example, in *The Tale of the Flopsy Bunnies*, Beatrix Potter says that 'the effect of eating too much lettuce is soporific' and both pictures and further text make it quite clear that the effect of too much lettuce on the Flopsy Bunnies has been to send them into such a deep and contented sleep that they don't notice when Mr McGregor picks them up by the ears and drops them all into a sack! Readers who have made themselves familiar with the book will know when a word that may be strange is coming up, so that the children listening can be observed to see if they are indeed puzzled, and will also know whether the next few sentences, or the pictures, make the meaning clear, so that it won't be necessary to interpolate an explanation of the new word's meaning into the reading. Similarly, a reader who knows the book well will be able to check on unusual grammar, which may be more confusing to the listeners than unusual vocabulary.

Sometimes books that might otherwise be attractive to children contain passages which may be of little interest to them. *Watership Down*, for example, has descriptions of the Sussex landscape, ecological discussions and scientific information about rabbits' behaviour, as well as the adventure story. Older readers may find these very rewarding – indeed it's not at all impossible that there are 4 year olds who delight in a detailed knowledge of rabbits, since there are so many children of that age who are dinosaur experts! – but teachers may be doubtful that such passages will hold the attention of most of their listeners. The judicious course seems to be to shorten them, or leave them out altogether; similarly, problematic vocabulary or grammar can be simplified. Changes like these can only be made sensibly if the 'editor' knows the book well enough to ensure that nothing crucial is left out or changed, and knows the audience well enough to guess what its interests, knowledge and attention span are likely to be.

If the teacher knows the book well, s/he can organise reading it so that the audience's interest is held and increased. Each day's reading might be preceded by a recapitulatory discussion of what has already happened in the story, and some guesses at what might happen next. These little sessions help children remember the past and predict the future, activities that contribute to feeling their way into the world of the story, and also allow them to practise the skills of linking past, present and future through memory and prediction, which are important parts of cognition more generally. Teachers can use them to motivate the audience to attend, just as editors do when they preface a magazine serial with a little summary of 'the story so far', which builds up to a crucial question and 'now read on'. In the same way, teachers reading a serial story may choose to end the day's instalment at a particularly exciting point, leaving the audience in suspense so that it will be eager to listen again tomorrow: Will the Flopsy Bunnies get out of the sack? Will Kehaar find the does? Will Dorothy and her friends get the lion out of the poppy field? Children can be asked to suggest how the characters should solve problems like these. Even at the nursery stage they can come up with lively – and often practicable – suggestions. For example, in the evaluation study the children offered the following suggestions for saving the sleeping lion from the deadly poppies: 'Pull out the poppies by handfuls', 'Cut down the poppies with the Tin Man's axe', 'Use a pipe to get him fresh air', and clearly enjoyed the challenge to solve the problem and express their own ideas.

Discussion of the book is an important part of literary theme development. Christianne Hayward used the story-telling times to talk about what happened and why, but, more interestingly, children in the evaluation study also brought up story issues and displayed story knowledge outside story time and even outside the nursery class. Parents were recruited to keep records of their children's remarks about books, and there were many instances of children using vocabulary drawn from the stories or comparing their own experience with something from the book. A child called Chris provides two vocabulary examples, as reported by his parents.

> 'His sister was asking us where foxes lived. Chris said he didn't know the answer to that but he remembered from *Watership Down* that rabbits live in warrens.'

> 'We were in the park today and we noticed that the river was very swollen and running very fast. Before I could

explain further, Chris said the movement of the river was called "current" and he knew this because he had heard it in *Watership Down*.'

These examples of extended vocabularies are typical: formal examination of the vocabulary children used in retelling favourite stories of their own choice showed that children who had taken part in the literary theme development programme used more different words and many more rare and infrequent words than children who had only had the ordinary nursery class exposure to books.

Besides vocabulary growth, children even at nursery age can draw appropriate analogies between the stories they hear and their own experience. Again, parents' records from the evaluation study provide many examples.

'Travelling in the car on the way to Bath, looking out over the countryside, Annie remarked that it looked just like the fields in *Watership Down* and asked if we could stop and look for rabbits. On the way back she said the rabbits were having their evening silflay.

The same child was heard to say to a friend, 'Alex, if you poke your eyes again, you'll look like General Woundwort with only one eye.'

Two school observations of Kenny:
'Kenny approaches with hand holding his forehead, "Miss Hayward, I've hurt myself bad, but don't worry, I'm Bigwig the strongest rabbit. I'm brave like Bigwig".'

Kenny is telling his teacher about an incident in *Watership Down*: '. . . there was the four Mark Captains and one – he had some does in his mouth. The four Mark Captains are strong – stronger than you are Mrs B., but not stronger than me 'cause I'm like Bigwig. I'm the *strongest* and *fastest*.'

The children in the evaluation study also showed an interest in relatively abstract issues which arose in the stories, clearly often thinking about them for some considerable time. For example, Tammy, a little girl whom both parents and teachers found difficult to handle, attention-seeking, 'silly' and 'shallow', came up with the question 'If Bigwig is so strong and Blackberry gets the brains, why is Hazel the leader?', *not* what one might expect as a question from a child not yet

$4\frac{1}{2}$. Three other little girls, playing in the imaginative play corner, which is arranged as Dorothy's house, put all the puppets along the walls with a blanket to cover their feet. They say: 'Every single puppet is in there, even the witch 'cause they're all friends. They're all babies so they don't hate each other yet.' It is important to emphasise that comments and questions like these were not exceptional – that throughout the evaluation study the children extended the story for themselves.

Christianne Hayward's programme used the other activities available in the classroom to reinforce and extend the story theme. Doing this capitalised on the children's interest in the story, and gave them materials, time and space to practise the new concepts they had met in it, with opportunities for experimentation, exploration and mastery. Some of the activities just used characters or settings from the stories – for example, jigsaw puzzles of the rabbits from *Watership Down* or sewing together fabric shapes to make a heart for the Tin Man from *The Wizard of Oz* – but others were more open-ended, allowing children to explore themes from the story as they thought fit. A chart of play activities linked to *Watership Down* illustrates the basic plan (see Figure 6.4). It is important to note that receiving and using ideas from children, parents and other staff is very much part of the ideology. The contents of the imaginative play corner, for example, were redesigned by the children into a place infinitely more stimulating than the ordinary Wendy House – and infinitely more productive of sophisticated language and role play.

The chart contains many suggestions for activities related to the story but within the overall structure of the nursery or infant classroom. The basic rationale for each type of activity will be familiar to teachers of young children. The curriculum available to children is not in its elements very different from the ordinary free play curriculum. However, there are three significant differences in its structure or organisation: first, the literary-related theme integrates the activities; second, it is run with more explicit mutual agreement on choice of activities between child and teacher; and third, it allows much more shared knowledge between child and teacher and hence much more genuine conversation and discussion.

The literary theme runs through all the activities on offer to the child. Instead of being what to the child is an arbitrary and unrelated menu, the activities have a common theme, which makes it easier for the child to know what to do with them. In the ordinary free play curriculum, children often seem not to know how to develop their play with the materials. They may flounder and not get very far, like the child at the water trough who just scooped up water and poured it out again as if she had no idea what else to do. Or they may use the material in one particular way, so that the activity becomes facile, no longer a challenge and no longer particularly rewarding. Kathy Sylva and her colleagues (Sylva *et al.*, 1980), and the Keele (Hutt, personal communication) and Open University (Meadows and Cashdan, 1983) studies, found that materials with some inherent structure produced more complex challenging play because the structure helped the child to progress and provided feedback information on whether things were going right. The literary theme running through activities that have less explicit goals gives children a similar sort of structure to hold on to and measure themselves against. When children have to invent their own goal as well as practising the skills of using the material, the goal is often not very ambitious. For example, they may play stereotyped 'mothers and fathers' in the Wendy House because this is one of the few themes familiar enough to be maintained while also sharing roles with other children, or they may make simple three-piece aeroplanes with construction material because they are easy to visualise and put together although a more elaborately constructed model would be preferred. When there is a tightly defined goal, as in a jigsaw puzzle or an arithmetic problem, they may be constrained by it and not develop the activity further. Using a theme or an example from a story means that the child does not have to invent the goal as well as working towards it, so that resources are freed to concentrate on the skills of the activity, *and* what is achieved is more than just having practised one's skills. The result in the evaluation study was that unfocused aimless play almost disappeared. Because the literary themes and examples are rich and complex – beyond what many adults could put together, let alone a young child – they paradoxically allow greater freedom than a narrower, more limited goal: the question of doing as well as the example, or of arriving at the goal, does not arise, precisely because it is too difficult to do so. You might wish to paint like Rembrandt, for example, but not blame yourself at all because you can't, whereas it is reasonable to feel a bit inadequate because you can't apply gloss paint to a door without getting runs in the paint or spots on your cuffs!

The context that the literary theme provides offers possible goals for play, ways of organising your activity, reasons for using your skills; and also more integration of different skills and activities than the ordinary free play curriculum allows because the different activities can all serve the same theme. The evaluation study children decided

Activities in the literary-centred curriculum: examples from the 'Watership Down' material

Activities/Materials	Sample possible objectives	Theme story adaptations
Reading	Reading Readiness Handling books Following text and pictures Vocabulary development Discussion of stories Use of reference books Participating in story sessions Independent reading	Provide several copies of theme book Provide fiction and nonfiction books related to theme book Provide pictures and text for making a story book (e.g. in a self-adhesive photo album)
Writing	Pencil/instrument control Letter awareness and formation Reading readiness Creative challenge Understanding written media Using functions of writing	Writing incidents in theme book (e.g. noticeboards) Messages, extensions of story etc. Free Design Provide stimulus, picture cards for copying etc.
Individualised project files	Independence Problem solving Writing, reading etc. Editing/discussing	Use theme book characters, situations and setting as basis for projects
Matching and puzzles	Visual discrimination, pattern making Problem solving, mathematical concepts Reading readiness	Use theme book characters, situations and setting as basis for projects
Music and Dance	Creative challenge, expression Cultural awareness	Make up new songs on Watership Down theme to old familiar tunes Discuss animal language e.g. rabbits thumping
PE and games	Small and large muscle control Social rules Strategy thinking	Adapt old games and revive new interest e.g. Rabbit Bingo. What's the time Captain Woundwort?
Sand	Problem solving Small muscle control Creative challenge	Free design Provide tube and water to make burrows Provide wooden rabbits (perhaps given distinguishing characteristics)

Water	Problem solving Small muscle control Creative challenge	Experiment with floating and sinking, current etc.
Science	Problem solving Small and large muscle control Number concept Observation and recording Instrument control	Use reference books Care for rabbit Study birds, insects, plants Grow plants, discuss wild versus tame issues Investigate rabbits' feeding, breeding, etc.
Wendy House/imaginative centre	Role playing Creative challenge Concept experimenting Free design (& Manufacture)	Develop props and setting as story progresses (e.g. provide burrow rabbit puppets, masks etc.)
Wood and nails Construction materials Clay Blocks	Large and small muscle control Instrument skills and control Free design Planning and sequencing Creating and finishing	Make rafts, hutches, boats etc. (Provide a variety of materials)
Sewing	Small muscle control Culture awareness Texture awareness Creative challenge Free design Planning and Sequencing Creating and Finishing	Applique, puppets, props, embroider round pictures etc.
Painting	Instrument control Creative challenge Self expression Cultural awareness Story recording	Children may find *illustrating* a story too challenging but always be ready to record a story and encourage free design
Reminders Children learn in different ways and at different rates. Children learn best when they are interested and not too uncertain. Children learn well when others are encouraging and involved.		Learning has to be learned: provide an environment that poses solveable problems for children and encourages discovery and recognition of solutions. Be aware of each child's social, physical, intellectual, cultural and emotional development.

the Watership Down corner needed glove puppets of *all* the named rabbits, for example, and insisted on making them by sewing scraps of felt or by drawing them on strong paper, using the picture book – and their own imaginations – as guides. Playing outside, they used the available crates, tyres and so forth as burrows and hutches, enacting the wild rabbits' rescue of the domesticated does – a role play that was a theme recurring over playtimes for a week or more. Fitting activities and materials to the needs of the play theme meant using them more creatively – and discussing them more – than the ordinary curriculum required.

Christianne Hayward also used the literary theme in her classroom in ways that gave the child the responsibility to make decisions and follow them through. Activities were designed for maximum child independence, with materials conveniently accessible so that children could select, use and clear away their own apparatus each time. Each activity had a record chart for staff to note which children had used it, so that a record of what each child did could be compiled. Each session, teacher and child discussed what activities the child should do that day, some activities being specially prepared for each child, and at least one being left to his or her own free choice. This preliminary negotiation meant that both teacher and children knew what each would be spending time on that day, and made it easier for children to plan their activities and structure their day. This procedure reduced both the amount of time children spent wandering around not knowing what to do and the amount of management the teacher had to do. Children enjoyed this little extra bit of certainty, since their choice of activities was not over-directed or constrained but it was easier for them to choose to do rewarding things. They also enjoyed the continuity that came from discussing with the teacher what they had done and what they might do tomorrow. With teacher and child sharing knowledge of the child's activities, there are more opportunities for sensible conversations rather than strained one-off comments on the lines of 'Oh, what a lovely picture', 'You have done that nicely – what are you going to do now?' and so on. There is also more to discuss with parents, and a sounder basis for assessments of the child's development, if these are needed.

The third 'structural' difference between the literary theme curriculum and the ordinary free play curriculum is that, because teacher and children both know the story, they have a shared topic for conversation. With a complex story such as *Watership Down*, *The Wizard of Oz* or *Heidi*, there is a great deal to talk about and many ways in which the story can be linked to other aspects of the child's (or the teacher's) experience. The potential for real, rich conversations is enormous; such conversations contribute to the children's language development and also give the teacher an ideal opportunity to assess the children's competence, to extend their knowledge and conceptualising and to motivate them towards working with the teacher and towards making use of books and stories. Christianne Hayward suggests that a love of literature is infectious and working with the literary theme curriculum helps children catch this infection. They may also 'catch' the idea that teachers are rewarding to talk to, an idea that the conventional free play curriculum certainly does not support.

CHAPTER 7

Summary and Conclusions

When we consider the curriculum of early childhood education we are confronted with questions of **'what?'**, **'how?'**, **'when?'**, **'why?'**, and **'with what effect?'**.

'**What?**' has different levels of answer: the micro-level of small and detailed activities – 'count to ten', 'tie his shoelaces' – through to the macro-level of social and cultural ideologies. In early childhood education we have a rich cafeteria spread of 'what to do', with less consideration of nutritional balance, size of portion, relative desirability of different components. Not surprisingly, teachers may despair at the impossible task of fitting everything in, and children may be overwhelmed into a restricted diet or teaspoonfuls of everything left barely tasted on the plate. Our curriculum innovations provide some coherence to the '**what?**', and make more explicit the nutritional principles, which are more important than any particular foodstuff.

The traditional answer to the '**how?**' has been 'through the child's own experience and activity', so that young children have been put in the position of being the major actors in choosing, organising, selecting and evaluating their own learning experiences, with little provision for them to learn by observation and even less opportunity to learn by being taught. We have argued that this practice is unbalanced, that it makes more psychological and ethnographic sense to recognise how much children learn as apprentices to the more expert, how crucial a 'Cognitive Advance Support System' is.* Our curricula spot-

*We have got used to Chomsky's postulated Language Acquisition Device or LAD, to which Bruner (1983) has added a Language Acquisition Support System. We have argued in this book for an analogous Cognitive Advance Support System: perhaps there might be room, still, for a neo-Piagetian CAD?

light the teacher's role here and provide a supportive context for the teaching–learning process.

As to 'when?': the traditional, largely Piagetian, answer has been that 'readiness is all'. We are not denying the strong maturational force behind children's development, which accelerates, constrains and directs their learning according to a schedule not determined by adults, but there are too many problems, both conceptual and moral, with the notion of 'readiness' for it to be a satisfactory answer to 'when?'. Our emphasis on a supportive and interactional curriculum whose principles apply to all learners, whatever their age and expertise, answers 'when?' with, approximately, 'when it is a matter of a small enjoyable effort'.

'Why?', here as elsewhere, is always the big question. One major conflict of ideas, pervading the whole of education, begins to surface even in the pre-school. It is the question of whether education is supposed to be good for the individuals receiving it or for the society providing it. Currently it is being said that schooling is primarily about preparing children to be useful, employable members of the future society. Society's needs, defined in terms of cultural and political issues, are seen as more important in the long term and even in the short term than the current needs and interests of children. Even young children are to be assessed, and schools are to be judged on the level their pupils have reached, not on the amount of progress they are making. Not so very long ago, a nursery school known to one of us was chided by a senior official for not having a higher level of attainment, and when it was pointed out that many pupils entered the school with a very low level of school-relevant skills the official recommended, apparently seriously, that such children should be excluded from the intake because they reduced the school's average. We are not arguing that education can be entirely individualistic, and we do not believe that society's needs should not be considered when the curriculum is set up and its success or failure examined. However, we are concerned that the child's potential must be considered as well as the child's actuality and society's needs. Our model of teaching and learning implies a gentle and supportive apprenticeship for children in the skills that schooling requires. Our curriculum innovations hope to facilitate this. And our answer to 'why this way?' is that we believe the approach combines effectiveness and caring in an optimum way.

This book has been largely about 'how?' and 'with what effect?'. We believe that the core of early childhood education must be fruitful discussion of the shared wisdom of teachers and learners, the teacher inducing the learner to move from being a spectator to being a reflective participant increasingly able to apply skills autonomously. We see the two curriculum innovations we described in Chapters 5 and 6 as two of several ways of doing this, each with its own considerable merits, each known to have operated successfully. We recommend them to readers as important parts of their strategies for helping young children learn.

Bibliography

Bennett, N. (1976) *Teaching style and pupil progress*. London: Open Books
Bennett, N., *et al.* (1984) *The quality of pupil learning experiences*. London: Erlbaum
Blank, M. (1973) *Teaching learning in the preschool: a dialogue approach*. Columbus, Ohio: Charles Merrill
Blank, M., *et al.* (1978) *The language of learning*. New York: Grune & Stratton
Bone, M. (1977) *Preschool children and the need for daycare*. OPCS Social Survey. London: HMSO
Brown, G., and Harris, T. (1978) *Social origins of depression*. London: Tavistock
Bruner, J. S. (1974) *The relevance of education*. Harmondsworth: Penguin
Bruner, J. S. (1980) *Under five in Britain*. London: Grant McIntyre
Bruner, J. S. (1983) *Child's talk: learning to use language*. Oxford: OUP
Burberry, R. (1980) 'An observational study of child and adult behaviour in preschool groups'. MEd dissertation, University of Bristol
Cashdan, A. (1986) *Literacy: teaching and learning language skills*. Oxford: Blackwell
Chi, M., and Koeske, R. (1983) 'Network representation of a child's dinosaur knowledge'. *Developmental Psychology*, 19(1): 29–39
Clark, M. M. (1976) *Young fluent readers*. London: Heinemann
Clark, M. M. (1988) *Children under five: educational research and evidence*. London: Gordon & Breach
Clark, M. M., and Cheyne, W. M. (eds) (1979) *Studies in preschool education*. London: Hodder & Stoughton
Clarke-Stewart, A. (1982) *Day care*. London: Fontana
Clay, M. M. (1979) *The early detection of reading difficulties: a diagnostic survey with recovery procedures*. London: Heinemann
Clement, J., *et al.* (1984) *Changed lives: the effects of the Perry Preschool Program on Youths through 19*. Ypsilanti, Michigan: High/Scope Press
Clift, P. (1980) *Aims, role and deployment of staff in the nursery*. Windsor: NFER
Curtis, A. (1985) *A curriculum for the preschool child*. Windsor: NFER–Nelson

Davie, C., *et al.* (1984) *The young child at home.* Windsor: NFER–Nelson

DES (1972) *Education: a framework for expansion* (White Paper). London: HMSO

Donaldson, M. (1978) *Children's minds.* London: Fontana

Dowling, M. (1988) *Education three to five: a teachers' handbook.* London: Paul Chapman Publishing

Dunn, J. (1984) *Sisters and brothers.* London: Open Books

Durkin, D. (1966) *Children who read early.* New York: Teachers' College Press

Eyken, W. van der (1982) *The education of three to eight year olds in the eighties.* Windsor: NFER

Eyken, W. van der, *et al.* (1984) 'Preschooling in Britain: a national study of institutional provision for under-fives in England, Scotland and Wales'. *Early Child Development and Care*, **17**(2): 79–122.

Fivush, R. (1984) 'Learning about school: the development of kindergarteners' school scripts'. *Child Development*, **55**: 1697–1709

Francis, H. (1982) *Learning to read.* London: Allen & Unwin

Galton, M., *et al.* (1980) *Inside the primary classroom.* London: Routledge

Hall, N. (1987) *The emergence of literacy.* London: Hodder & Stoughton

Hayward, C. (1982a) 'Literary theme development in the nursery'. *Tutors of Advanced Courses for Teachers of Young Children Journal*, **2**(2): 30–40

Hayward, C. (1982b) 'Literary theme development in the nursery classroom'. MEd thesis, University of Bristol

Heath, S. B. (1983) *Ways with words.* Cambridge: CUP

Hess, R. D. and Shipman, V. C. (1965) 'Early experience and the socialisation of cognitive modes in children'. *Child Development*, **36**: 869–86

Hewison, J., and Tizard, J. (1980) 'Parental involvement and reading attainment'. *British Journal of Educational Psychology*, **50**: 209–15

Hohmann, M., *et al.* (1979) *Young children in action.* Ypsilanti: High/Scope Press

Hughes, M., *et al.* (1980) *Nurseries now.* Harmondsworth: Penguin Books

Hunt, J. McV. (1969) *The challenge of incompetence and poverty.* Chicago: University of Illinois Press

Jensen, A. R. (1969) 'How much can we boost IQ and scholastic achievement?' *Harvard Educational Review*, **39**: 1–123

Jowett, S., and Sylva, K. (1986) 'Does kind of preschool matter?' *Educational Research*, **28**(1): 23–31

Lazar, I., and Darlington, R. (1982) 'Lasting effects of early education: a report from the Consortium for Longitudinal Studies'. *Monographs of the Society for Research in Child Development*, Serial No. 195, 47

Lomax, C. (1977) 'Interest in books and stories at nursery school'. *Educational Research*, **IX**(2): 100–12

Mably, S. (1977) 'Observations of a group of nursery school children in relation to parental attitude towards Nursery Education'. BEd dissertation, Hatfield Polytechnic

Meadows, S. (ed.) (1983) *Developing thinking.* London: Methuen

Meadows, S. (1986) *Understanding child development.* London: Hutchinson.

Meadows, S., and Cashdan, A. (1979) 'Matching the child's level: one aspect of a British Pre-School Intervention Study'. In R. E. Schafer (ed.) *Applied Linguistics & Reading.* International Reading Association

Meadows, S., and Cashdan, A. (1983) *Teaching styles in nursery education: final reportt to SSRC*

Meadows, S., Mills, M., and Puckering, C. (1987) 'Mother–child interaction and its shortterm and longterm outcomes in depressed and non-depressed women'. Paper given at the British Psychological Society Developmental Section Conference, York, September

Moore, E., and Smith, T. (1987) *One year on: High/Scope Report 2*. London: VOLCUF

Nash, R. (1974) *Classrooms observed*. London: Routledge

Nelson, K. (1986) *Event knowledge: structure and function in development*. Hillsdale, NJ: Erlbaum

New, C., and David, M. (1985) *For the children's sake*. Harmondsworth: Penguin

Nisbet, J., and Shucksmith, J. (1986) *Learning strategies*. London: Routledge

Osborn, A. F. (1981) 'Under-fives in school in England and Wales 1971-9'. *Educational Research*, **23**(2): 96-103

Osborn, A. F., and Milbank, J. E. (1987) *The effects of early education*. Oxford: OUP

Osborn, A. F., *et al.* (1984) *The social life of Britain's five year olds*. London: Routledge

Rutter, M. (1981) *Maternal deprivation reassessed*. Harmondsworth: Penguin

Schiff, M., *et al.* (1986) *Education and class: the irrelevance of IQ genetic studies*. Oxford: Clarendon Press

Schweinhart, L. J., and Weikart, D. (1980) *Young children grow up: the effects of the Perry Preschool Program on youths through age 15*. Ypsilanti: High/Scope Press

Smilansky, S. (1968) *The effects of sociodramatic play on disadvantaged pre-school children*. New York: Wiley

Smith, P. K. (1988) 'Children's play and its role in early development: a re-evaluation of the "play ethos" '. In A. D. Pellegrini (ed.) *Psychological bases for early education*. Chichester: Wiley

Sylva, K., *et al.* (1980) *Child watching at playgroup and nursery school*. London: Grant McIntyre

Sylva, K., *et al.* (1986) *Monitoring the High/Scope Training Programme*. London: VOLCUF

Tizard, B. (1975) *Early Childhood Education: a review and discussion of current research in Britain*. Windsor: NFER

Tizard, B., and Hughes, M. (1984) *Young children learning*. London: Fontana

Tizard, B., *et al.* (1976a) 'Staff behaviour in preschool centres'. *Journal of Child Psychology and Psychiatry*, **17**: 21-33

Tizard, B. *et al.* (1976b) 'Play in preschool centres: I Play measures and their relation to age, sex and IQ'. *Journal of Child Psychology and Psychiatry*, **17**: 251-64

Tizard, B., *et al.* (1976c) 'Play in preschool centres. II Effects on play of the child's social class and of the educational orientation of the centre'. *Journal of Child Psychology and Psychiatry*, **17**: 265-74

Tizard, B., *et al.* (1982) 'Adults' cognitive demands at home and at nursery school'. *Journal of Child Psychology and Psychiatry*, **23**: 105-16

Tizard, B., *et al.* (1988) *Young children at school in the inner city.* London: Erlbaum

Vygotsky, L. (1978) *Mind in society* (ed. Cole). Harvard: Harvard University press

Wadsworth, M. (1986) 'Effects of parenting style and preschool experience on children's verbal attainment: results of a British longitudinal study'. *Early Childhood Research Quarterly*, 1

Weikart, D., *et al.* (1978) *Ypsilanti Preschool Curriculum Demonstration Project.* Ypsilanti: High/Scope Press

Wells, G. (1981) *Learning through interaction.* Cambridge: CUP

Wells, G. (1985) *Language development in the preschool years.* Cambridge: CUP

Wells, G. (1986) *The meaning makers.* London: Hodder & Stoughton

Wilson, M. (1982) 'Classroom activities in an infant school'. MEd dissertation, University of Bristol

Wood, D. (1986) 'Aspects of learning and teaching'. In M. Richards and P. Light (eds) *Children of social worlds.* Cambridge: Polity Press

Wood, D. (1988) *How children think and learn.* Oxford: Blackwell

Wood, D., *et al.* (1980) *Working with under fives.* London: Grant McIntyre

Woodhead, M. (1976) *Intervening in disadvantage: a challenge for nursery education.* Windsor: NFER

Woodhead, M. (1983) 'Preschool education has long-term effects – but can they be generalised?' *Oxford Review of Education*, 11: 133–55

Woodhead, M. (1988a) 'School starts at five . . . or four years old? The rationale for changing admission policies in England and Wales'. *Journal of Educational Policy* (forthcoming)

Woodhead, M. (1988b) 'When Psychology informs public policy: the case of early childhood intervention'. *American Psychologist* (forthcoming)

Zigler, E., and Valentine, J. (eds) (1979) *Project Head Start: a legacy of the war on poverty.* New York: The Free Press

Index